Injia on Coronial Proceedings in Papua New Guinea and the Pacific

Salamo Injia

University of Papua New Guinea Press and Bookshop, 2013

Injia on Coronial Proceedings in Papua New Guinea and the Pacific

ISBN: 978-9980-945-98-3

PUBLISHED BY:
The University of Papua New Guinea Press and Bookshop
PO Box 413
University PO, NCD
Papua New Guinea
Email: upngpress@gmail.com

FOREWORD

This textbook is one of eight (8) textbooks written under my hand and supervision:

'Injia on Criminal Offences in Papua New Guinea and the Pacific'

'Injia on Criminal Practice and Procedure in Papua New Guinea and the Pacific'

'Injia on Sentencing in Papua New Guinea and the Pacific'

'Injia on Statutory Interpretation in Papua New Guinea and the Pacific'

'Injia on Coronial Proceedings in Papua New Guinea and the Pacific'

'Injia on Investigatory Practice in Papua New Guinea and the Pacific'

'Injia on Contempt of Court in Papua New Guinea and the Pacific'

'Injia on Evidence in Papua New Guinea and the Pacific'

Each of those textbooks is an effort to offer to Judicial officers, legal practitioners and students of law a comprehensive set of principles and practical guidelines on criminal law and practice in Papua New Guinea and the Pacific. The work undertaken under the auspices of AusAID through the PNG-Australia Law and Justice Partnership Project is an extension of a similar project undertaken previously in writing the textbook *Criminal Law and Practice in Papua New Guinea* co-authored by myself, Professor Don Chalmers, Dr Weisbrot and Justice Andrew.

The textbooks will be of great benefit to the criminal justice system in Papua New Guinea and the Pacific and specifically will assist judges, magistrates, lawyers, law students and police officers in the performance of their duties.

The assistance of AusAID and its development practitioner Mr Errol Gibson who provided research and spent countless hours in the production of these textbooks is acknowledged.

Sir Salamo Injia, Kt

Chief Justice of Papua New Guinea

22nd September 2013

TABLE OF CONTENTS

		Page
PREFACE		
INTRODUCTION		1
APPOINTMENT OF A CORONER		19
DEATH INQUEST		
[1.0]	**Introduction**	21
[2.0]	**Jurisdiction**	23
[3.0]	**No Inquest**	25
[4.0]	**Initial Report**	28
[5.0]	**View**	31
[6.0]	**Non-Suspicious And Non-Unusual Death**	31
[7.0]	**Investigation**	32
[8.0]	**Investigation File**	
[8.1]	Contents	34
[8.2]	Copies	38
[8.3]	Investigating Officer's Statement	38
[9.0]	**Death In Custody**	
[9.1]	Introduction	40
[9.2]	Investigation	42
[9.3]	Duty Of Care	44
[9.4]	Avoidable Harm	45
[9.5]	Brutality	45

TABLE OF CONTENTS

		Page
[10.0]	**Identification Of A Deceased Person**	
[10.1]	Who Should Identify A Deceased Person	45
[10.2]	Methods Of Identification	
[10.2.1]	Introduction	46
[10.2.2]	Fingerprints	47
[10.2.3]	Dental Records	47
[10.2.4]	Distinctive Markings	47
[10.2.5]	Personal Property	48
[10.2.6]	DNA Test	48
[10.2.7]	X-Rays	48
[10.2.8]	Personal Identification Documentation	49
[11.0]	**Post-Mortem Examination**	49
[12.0]	**Burial**	55
[13.0]	**Exhumation**	56
FIRE INQUEST		
[1.0]	**Introduction**	58
[2.0]	**Initial Report**	61
[3.0]	**Investigation**	62
[4.0]	**Investigation File**	
[4.1]	Contents	63
[4.2]	Copies	65
[4.3]	Investigating Officer's Statement	66
MISSING PERSON INQUEST		
[1.0]	**Introduction**	67
[2.0]	**Investigation File**	
[2.1]	Contents	68
[2.2]	Copies	69
[2.3]	Investigating Officer's Statement	70

TABLE OF CONTENTS

		Page
WITNESS ATTENDANCE		71
COURT PROCEDURE		
[1.0]	**Introduction**	75
[2.0]	**Open Court**	78
[3.0]	**Media**	79
[4.0]	**Rules Of Evidence**	81
[5.0]	**Rules Of Natural Justice**	83
[6.0]	**Coroner's Assistant**	86
[7.0]	**Interested Party**	88
[8.0]	**Oath, Solemn Declaration And Affirmation**	93
[9.0]	**Competency And Compellability**	
[9.1]	Death And Fire Coronial Inquest	94
[9.2]	Missing Person Coronial Inquest	96
[10.0]	**Privilege Against Self-Incrimination**	97
[11.0]	**Protection Of Witnesses**	98
[12.0]	**Examination Of Witnesses**	99
[13.0]	**Statements And Reports**	104
FINDINGS		
[1.0]	**Introduction**	106
[2.0]	**Standard Of Proof**	110

TABLE OF CONTENTS

		Page
[3.0]	**Death Inquest**	
[3.1]	Introduction	112
[3.2]	No Death	113
[3.3]	Death Uncertain	113
[3.4]	Open Finding	113
[3.5]	Natural Causes	115
[3.6]	Suicide	115
[3.7]	Neglect	118
[3.8]	Accidental Death	119
[3.9]	Misadventure	
[3.9.1]	Generally	122
[3.9.2]	Medical Misadventure	122
[3.10]	Traffic Accident	123
[3.11]	Killed Unlawfully	124
[3.12]	Killed Lawfully	
[3.12.1]	Constitutional Provisions	127
[3.12.2]	Acting In Self Defence	129
[3.12.3]	Effect An Arrest	130
[3.12.4]	Prevent An Arrest	131
[3.12.5]	Suppress A Riot, Insurrection Or Mutiny	132
[3.12.6]	Preventing An Excape	133
[3.12.7]	Wording	134
[4.0]	**Fire Inquest**	135
[5.0]	**Missing Person Inquest**	137
COMMENTS AND RECOMMENDATIONS		
[1.0]	**Generally**	141
[2.0]	**Death Inquests Specifically**	142
EXHIBITS		144
CONTEMPT OF COURT		145
RE-OPENING		146

TABLE OF CONTENTS

		Page
JUDICIAL REVIEW		147
GLOSSARY OF MEDICAL TERMS		153
APPENDICES		
Appendix 1	'Initial Report Of Death To Coroner' Form	175
Appendix 2	'Initial Report Of Fire To Coroner' Form	178
INDEX		181

INTRODUCTION

The appellations 'Coronaries', 'Coronation' and 'Coruna' were used in statutes until the term 'Coroner' first appeared in the 14th century in England. However, the office is known to have existed as early as the 12th century and there is evidence that officers having powers similar to those of Coroners were in existence before then.[1]

In the early years the Coroner's duties were mainly administrative. He kept the King's records, particularly those relating to the criminal courts. He collected and guarded what were termed the 'chance' revenues trove and forfeited property of felons. Deodands were chattels which had caused the death of a human being, such as swords or carts or oxen. At first, the article or animal itself was forfeited, for religious purposes. Subsequently it became the task of the Coroner to assess its value, and collect that amount in coin. The more serious crimes became known as felonies. These included homicide, rape, arson, burglary, robbery, mayhem and larceny.

Barbarous physical punishments were inflicted for these offences, and the lands and goods of the felon were forfeited either to his lord or the King, under the supervision of the Coroner.

If a person was found dead, the Coroner was notified and a jury assembled from the local hundred. The body was lain on a table or board and examined by the jury under the direction of the Coroner. Evidence was heard and the jury's verdict taken. If a verdict of Manslaughter was returned, the accused, being present, was held for trial. At a subsequent conviction, the Coroner seized his property for the King. If the named offender was absent when the Coroner's jury, or grand jury, returned its finding, the local populace would set after him with hue and cry.

---

[1] This section is adopted from the 'Final Report of the Court Restructure Committee to the Chief Justice and the Chief Magistrate on the Coroner', dated 30th October 1996, NJSS Publication, Port Moresby. The Committee comprised of the Honorable Justice Timothy Hinchliffe CBE, as Chairman, and members the Honorable Justice Warrick Andrew CBE, the Honorable Justice Salamo Injia, the Honorable Justice Paul Akuram and Senior Magistrate Silas Samuel.

As to the historical development of the Office of Coroner, see also: *X v Deputy State Coroner for New South Wales* (2001) 51 NSWLR 312, [2001] NSWSC 46; *Josephine Conway v Mary Jerram, Magistrate and New South Wales State Coroner and another* [2010] NSWSC 371 and New Zealand Law Commission, 1999, 'Coroner A Review A Discussion Paper', Preliminary Paper 36, page 32.

INTRODUCTION

The Coroner also enquired into allegations of arson, mortal woundings and rape. His hearing was called 'Inquisto', hence the modern inquest.

The statute 'De Offico Coronatioris' (1276) sets out in detail the legal responsibilities of the Coroner:

> 'The Coroner should go to the places where any person is slain, or suddenly dead or wounded, or where homes are broken, or where treasure is said to be found, and should by his warrant to bailiffs or constables summon a jury of the four or five or six neighbouring towns to make inquiry upon view of the body; and the Coroner and jury should inquire into the manner of killing and all circumstances that occasioned the party's death; who were present, whether the dead person was known and where he lay the night before; they should examine the body to see if there be any signs of strangling about the neck, or of cords about the members, or burns. Also weapons should be viewed and inquiry made with what weapons. And the Coroner may send his warrant for witnesses, and take their examination in writing, and if any appear guilty of the murder he should inquire what goods, corn and land he had; and then the dead body should be buried. A Coroner may likewise commit the person to prison who is by his inquisition found guilty of the murder; and the witnesses should be bound by recognisances to appear at the next assizes'.

In modern times, the powers and duties of the Coroner are governed by the *Coroners Act* (Ch. 32).

A Coroner holding a coronial inquest has powers based on the common law and extended in some directions and limited in others by statute.[2]

---

[2] See Halsbury's Statutes of England, 3rd edition, Volume 7, page 235.

INTRODUCTION

Subject to the *Coroners Act* (Ch. 32), a Coroner has all the jurisdiction, power and authority that belongs to the office of a Coroner in England when holding a coronial inquest.[3]

The Coroners Court must act within the parameters of its enabling legislation.[4] Accordingly, in order to amount to a proper assumption of jurisdiction and exercise of it, there must be adherence to the requirements of the *Coroners Act* (Ch. 32).[5]

Lack of procedure can be addressed by way of Regulations as provided for by section 35 of the *Coroners Act* (Ch. 32).[6]

As a matter of practice all coronial inquests under the *Coroners Act* (Ch. 32) are conducted by a Magistrate.

The term 'inquest' means a coronial inquest or inquiry under the *Coroners Act* (Ch. 32).[7]

Therefore, the term 'inquest' covers:

- an inquest held into:
  - the 'manner';

    and

---

[3] See section 6 of the *Coroners Act* (Ch. 32).

[4] See *Aviat Social and Sporting Club (Lae) Inc v Anthony Meehan Ltd* (2001) N2071 and *Samson Dacany v Noah Taia of The National Fisheries Authority* (2002) N2316.

[5] See *Sakawar Kasieng v Andrew Baigry, Magistrate of Wewak District Court and The State* (2004) N2562.

[6] It should be noted that section 185 of the *Constitution of the Independent State of Papua New Guinea* only applies to the Supreme Court and the National Court.

[7] See section 1 of the *Coroners Act* (Ch. 32).

- the 'medical cause'

of the death of a deceased person[8];

- an inquest held into:
  - the 'cause';

    and
  - the 'origin'

of a fire[9];

and

- an inquiry held into:
  - the cause;

    and
  - circumstances

of the disappearance of a missing person[10].

The *Coroners Act* (Ch. 32) does not cover any other matters.[11]

---

[8] See section 7 of the *Coroners Act* (Ch. 32).

[9] See sections 17 and 18 of the *Coroners Act* (Ch. 32).

[10] See section 20 of the *Coroners Act* (Ch. 32).

[11] See *Nells Aingiris for himself and on behalf of 14 others v Orim Karapo and The State* (2008) N3325.

INTRODUCTION

A coronial inquest may be held into multiple deaths or missing persons, provided that the 'manner' and 'cause' of the deaths or the cause and circumstances of the disappearance of the missing persons are related.

For example, this may occur when an explosion occurs in a crowded building causing a fire and the consequent death of multiple persons, or where there is a major motor vehicle or aircraft accident.

A coronial inquest shall be held by a Coroner sitting alone.[12]

The purposes for holding a coronial inquest include:

- to make:
    - findings;
    - comments;

      and
    - recommendations

  in relation to the facts surrounding a death or fire or the disappearance of a missing person;
- to provide a public forum for considering public issues, including health or safety, in relation to a specific death or fire or the disappearance of a missing person;
- to allay rumours and suspicion in relation to a specific death[13];

[12] See section 5 of the *Coroners Act* (Ch. 32).

[13] See *R v Greater Manchester Coroner; ex parte Tal* [1985] QB 67 at 83.

and

- where necessary to commit a person to stand trial in the National Court.

It is however not a purpose of holding a coronial inquest:

- to provide a forum for attempts to gather evidence for pending or future criminal or civil[14] proceedings[15];

  or

- to determine litigated rights[16].

A coronial inquest does not necessarily have to be held in a courthouse.

Where a person dies in circumstances as specified in section 7 of the *Coroners Act* (Ch. 32) a Coroner has jurisdiction to inquire into the manner and cause of the death.

A Coroner may hold a coronial inquest where:

- he or she is of the opinion that a coronial inquest ought to be held;

  or

---

[14] See *Huynh and Huynh v Dr. Jones et al* (1991) 2 OR (3d) 562, per McRuer CJ at 565.

[15] See *Poplar Coroner; ex parte Thomas* [1993] QB 610, [1993] 2 All ER 381, per Dillcn LJ at 629 and 387.

[16] See *R v Hocken; ex parte Jenkins* (1876) 1 NZ Jurist. Rep (N.S.) 121 at 127 and *S v The Director of Public Prosecutions and others* [2007] ACTSC 100.

- a person authorised by section 21(2)(b) of the *Coroners Act* (Ch. 32) requests him or her to hold a coronial inquest.[17]

  The authorised persons are the Commissioner of Police, a Superintendent of Police and the husband, wife, father, mother, sister, brother, son, daughter or guardian of a deceased person.[18]

  Before holding a coronial inquest at the request of an authorised person, a Coroner may require a written statement of the grounds for the request.[19]

  Where a Coroner considers that such grounds do not warrant the holding of a coronial inquest he or she may refuse to hold it, but the Coroner shall in writing accompanied by a copy of the grounds as to his or her refusal inform the Attorney-General.[20]

Whenever a person dies:

- in a correctional institution[21];
- in a rural lock-up[22];
- in a police lock-up[23];

---

[17] See section 21(2) of the *Coroners Act* (Ch. 32).

[18] See section 21(5) of the *Coroners Act* (Ch. 32).

[19] See section 21(3) of the *Coroners Act* (Ch. 32).

[20] See section 21(4) of the *Coroners Act* (Ch. 32).

[21] See section 63 of the *Correctional Service Act 1995*.

[22] See section 64 of the *Correctional Service Act 1995*.

[23] See section 65 of the *Correctional Service Act 1995*.

- while a prisoner;

  or

- whilst in custody[24]

a coronial inquest should ordinarily be held.[25]

A Coroner shall inquire into the cause and origin of any fire by which any property has been destroyed or damaged where:

- he or she is of the opinion that a coronial inquest ought to be held;

  or

- the Attorney-General directs him or her to hold a coronial inquest.[26]

Furthermore, where:

- a person has been reported to a police officer as missing and the police have not found the missing person within the period of six months after the date of the report;

- a Coroner is of the opinion that a coronial inquest into the disappearance of a missing person ought to be held;

- the Attorney-General directs a Coroner to hold a coronial inquest into the disappearance of a missing person;

---

[24] See section 7(1)(h) of the *Coroners Act* (Ch. 32).

[25] See International Human Rights Instrument titled 'Body of Principals for the Protection of All Persons under Any Form of Detention or Imprisonment' -- Principal 34.

[26] See section 17 of the *Coroners Act* (Ch. 32).

or

- the Commissioner of Police, a Superintendent of Police or the husband, wife, father, mother, sister, brother, son, daughter or guardian of a missing person[27] requests a Coroner to hold a coronial inquest into that person's disappearance

a Coroner shall inquire into:

- the cause and circumstances of the disappearance of the missing person;

  and

- all matters and things that will reveal, or are likely to reveal, whether the missing person is alive or dead,

and if the person is:

- alive;

  or

- likely to be alive,

his or her whereabouts at the time of the inquest.[28]

It is desirable, but not a legal necessity, that due public notice of the holding of a coronial inquest should be given.[29]

---

[27] See section 20(5) of the *Coroners Act* (Ch. 32).

[28] See section 20(1) of the *Coroners Act* (Ch. 32).

[29] See Jervis on Coroners, 10th edition, page 138.

INTRODUCTION

The Bougainville Police Service and the Royal Papua New Guinea Constabulary are required to thoroughly investigate all potential coronial matters and report such matters to a Coroner.

A Coroner has an unrestricted power to investigate that which needs to be investigated.[30]

The role of a Coroner holding a coronial inquest is a hybrid process containing:

- an inquisitorial[31] element;

  and

- an adversarial element.[32]

---

[30] *See Harmsworth v The State Coroner* [1989] VR 989.

[31] The Coroner determines which witnesses are to be cross-examined.

See *The State v Jacob Toroken, Coroner; ex parte George Nelson Perera* (1981) N281.

See also: *R v Her Majesty's Coroner for North Humberside and Scunthorpe; ex parte Jamieson* [1995] QB 1 at 17, (1994) 158 JP 1011; *R v South London Coroner; ex parte Thompson* (1982) 126 SJ 625 and *McKerr v Armagh Coroner and others* [1990] 1 All ER 865 at 868-870.

[32] See *Musumeci v Attorney-General of New South Wales and another* (2003) 57 NSWLR 193, [2003] NSWCA 77; *R v South London Coroner; ex parte Thompson* (1982) 126 SJ 625; *Annetts v McCann* (1990) 170 CLR 596, [1990] HCA 57; *Fairfax Publications Pty Ltd v Abernethy* [1999] NSWSC 826; *Maksimovich v Walsh* [1985] 4 NSWLR 318, per Kirby P at 327-328 and Samuels JA at 337; *Mirror Newspapers Limited v Waller* [1985] 1 NSWLR 1 at 6 and *Herron v Attorney General for New South Wales* (1987) 8 NSWLR 601, per Kirby P at 608.

INTRODUCTION

Whilst a coronial inquest is not a judicial proceeding[33] a Coroner exercises judicial power[34], notwithstanding the executive nature of their functions[35].

However, a coronial inquest involves the administration of justice.[36]

A coronial inquest is a fact-finding exercise[37] in which there is:

- no charge[38];

---

[33] See *R v West London Coroner; ex parte Gray* [1988] QB 467, per Watkins LJ at 473.

[34] See *R v Electricity Commissioners; ex parte London Electricity Joint Committee Co (1920) Ltd* [1924] 1 KB 171.

See also: *Musumeci v Attorney-General of New South Wales and another* (2003) 57 NSWLR 193, [2003] NSWCA 77, per Ipp JA with whom Beazley JA agreed and *Harmsworth v The State Coroner* [1989] VR 989.

[35] See *Musumeci v Attorney-General of New South Wales and another* (2003) 57 NSWLR 193, [2003] NSWCA 77; *R v South London Coroner; ex parte Thompson* (1982) 126 SJ 625; *Annetts v McCann* (1990) 170 CLR 596, [1990] HCA 57; *Fairfax Publications Pty Ltd v Abernethy* [1999] NSWSC 826; *Maksimovich v Walsh* [1985] 4 NSWLR 318, per Kirby P at 327-328 and Samuels JA at 337; *Mirror Newspapers Limited v Waller* [1985] 1 NSWLR 1 at 6; *Herron v Attorney General for New South Wales* (1987) 8 NSWLR 601, per Kirby P at 608 and *Harmsworth v The State Coroner* [1989] VR 989.

[36] See *Musumeci v Attorney-General of New South Wales and another* (2003) 57 NSWLR 193, [2003] NSWCA 77; *R v South London Coroner; ex parte Thompson* (1982) 126 SJ 625; *Annetts v McCann* (1990) 170 CLR 596, [1990] HCA 57; *Fairfax Publications Pty Ltd v Abernethy* [1999] NSWSC 826; *Maksimovich v Walsh* [1985] 4 NSWLR 318, per Kirby P at 327-328 and Samuels JA at 337; *Mirror Newspapers Limited v Waller* [1985] 1 NSWLR 1 at 6 and *Herron v Attorney General for New South Wales* (1987) 8 NSWLR 601, per Kirby P at 608.

[37] See *The Coroner's Court v Newton* [2006] NZLR 312 at 319-320.

See also: New Zealand Law Commission, 1999, 'Coroner A Review A Discussion Paper', Preliminary Paper 36, page 1 and New Zealand Law Commission, 2000, 'Coroners', Report 62, page 3.

[38] See *The Coroner's Court v Newton* [2006] NZLR 312 at 319-320.

- no parties[39];

  and

- no trial[40],

but simply an attempt to establish facts[41], whilst not

- proportioning guilt[42];

  or

- determining civil liability[43].

---

[39] See *Annetts v McCann* (1990) 170 CLR 596 at 598, [1990] HCA 57; *R v South London Coroner; ex parte Thompson* (1982) 126 SJ 625; *R v Her Majesty's Coroner for North Humberside and Scunthorpe; ex parte Jamieson* [1995] QB 1 at 17, (1994) 158 JP 1011 and *The Coroner's Court v Newton* [2006] NZLR 312 at 319-320.

[40] See *Annetts v McCann* (1990) 170 CLR 596 at 598, [1990] HCA 57; *R v South London Coroner; ex parte Thompson* (1982) 126 SJ 625; *R v Her Majesty's Coroner for North Humberside and Scunthorpe; ex parte Jamieson* [1995] QB 1 at 17, (1994) 158 JP 1011 and *The Coroner's Court v Newton* [2006] NZLR 312 at 319-320.

See also: New Zealand Law Commission, 1999, 'Coroner A Review A Discussion Paper', Preliminary Paper 36, page 1 and New Zealand Law Commission, 2000, 'Coroners', Report 62, page 3.

[41] See *Annetts v McCann* (1990) 170 CLR 596 at 598, [1990] HCA 57 and *R v South London Coroner; ex parte Thompson* (1982) 126 SJ 625.

[42] See *Annetts v McCann* (1990) 170 CLR 596 at 598, [1990] HCA 57; *The Coroner's Court v Newton* [2006] NZLR 312 at 319-320 and *R v West London Coroner; ex parte Gray and others* [1987] 2 All ER 129 at 133.

See also: New Zealand Law Commission, 1999, 'Coroner A Review A Discussion Paper', Preliminary Paper 36, page 1 and New Zealand Law Commission, 2000, 'Coroners', Report 62, page 3.

[43] See *Huynh and Huynh v Dr. Jones et al* (1991) 2 OR (3d) 562, per McRuer CJ at 565.

INTRODUCTION

The question of civil liability is not an issue for a Coroner's Court to decide.[44]

It is not the function of a Coroner holding a coronial inquest to:

- determine, or appear to determine, any question of civil liability;

- apportion guilt;

  or

- attribute blame.[45]

The Coroner's Court is not the proper place to explore questions of clinical negligence and it is axiomatic that a coronial inquest should not be used as a stepping stone to civil litigation.[46]

---

[44] See *R v North Humberside and Scunthorpe Coroner; ex parte Jamieson* [1995] QB 1 at 23, (1994) 158 JP 1011; *R v Her Majesty's Coroner for Birmingham; ex parte Cotton* (1995) 160 JP 123; *R v Her Majesty's Coroner for North Humberside and Scunthorpe; ex parte Jamieson* [1995] QB 1, (1994) 158 JP 1011 and *R v Her Majesty's Coroner for Inner South London District; ex parte Epsom Health Care NHS Trust* (1993) 158 JP 973 at 978.

See also: The Function of the Coroner and the Coronial Jurisdiction; www.courts.act.gov.au.

[45] See *R v Her Majesty's Coroner for Birmingham; ex parte Cotton* (1995) 160 JP 123; *R v Her Majesty's Coroner for North Humberside and Scunthorpe; ex parte Jamieson* [1995] QB 1, (1994) 158 JP 1011 and *R v Her Majesty's Coroner for Inner South London District; ex parte Epsom Health Care NHS Trust* (1993) 158 JP 973 at 978.

[46] See *R v Her Majesty's Coroner for Birmingham; ex parte Cotton* (1995) 160 JP 123; *R v Her Majesty's Coroner for North Humberside and Scunthorpe; ex parte Jamieson* [1995] QB 1, (1994) 158 JP 1011 and *R v Her Majesty's Coroner for Inner South London District; ex parte Epsom Health Care NHS Trust* (1993) 158 JP 973 at 978.

INTRODUCTION

A coronial inquest is an inquisitorial process, a process of investigation quite unlike a trial[47].[48]

The procedures and rules of evidence suitable for a trial are unsuitable for a coronial inquest.[49]

The fact that cross-examination is permitted by interested parties with the consent of the Coroner does not detract from the inquisitorial nature of the process, and nor from the fact that the findings are not conclusive as to civil or criminal liability of any person.[50]

Whilst no person is liable to be convicted and punished in a coronial inquest, a witness may be convicted for failing to comply with specific provisions of the *Coroners Act* (Ch. 32)[51].[52]

A coronial inquest must never be used as part of the machinery for investigating crime.[53]

---

[47] See New Zealand Law Commission, 1999, 'Coroner A Review A Discussion Paper', Preliminary Paper 36, page 2.

[48] See *Annetts v McCann* (1990) 170 CLR 596 at 598, [1990] HCA 57; *R v South London Coroner; ex parte Thompson* (1982) 126 SJ 625 and *The Coroner's Court v Newton* [2006] NZLR 312 at 319-320.

See also: New Zealand Law Commission, 1999, 'Coroner A Review A Discussion Paper', Preliminary Paper 36, page 2 and New Zealand Law Commission, 2000, 'Coroners', Report 62, page 3.

[49] See *R v Her Majesty's Coroner for North Humberside and Scunthorpe; ex parte Jamieson* [1995] QB 1 at 17, (1994) 158 JP 1011 and *R v South London Coroner; ex parte Thompson* (1982) 126 SJ 625.

[50] See *The Coroner's Court v Newton* [2006] NZLR 312 at 319-320.

[51] See sections 26 and 28 of the *Coroners Act* (Ch. 32).

[52] As commented by Lord Bingham in *R v Davis* [2008] HRLR 35, [2008] 3 WLR 125, [2008] UKHL 36, [2008] 2 Cr App R 33, [2008] 3 All ER 461, [2008] Crim LR 415, [2008] 1 AC 1128.

[53] See *Attorney-General v Maksimovich* [1985] 4 NSWLR 300.

See also: *R v Bevan Spencer von Emein* [1991] SASC 2740.

INTRODUCTION

Whilst it must be conceded that much of the investigation is dealt with by the police in their ordinary duties, at the same time a coronial inquest affords a ready means of public investigation in cases:

- of suspicious crime;

  or

- affecting the public at large.[54]

A Coroner will fail in his or her duty if his or her investigation is:

- superficial;
- slipshod;

  or

- perfunctory.[55]

It is ultimately the responsibility of the Coroner to ensure that the relevant facts are:

- fully;
- fairly;

  and

---

[54] See Halsbury's Statutes of England, 3rd edition, Volume 7, page 236.

[55] See *R v Her Majesty's Coroner of North Humberside and Scunthorpe; ex parte Jamieson* [1995] QB 1 at 26, (1994) 158 JP 1011 at 1035.

See also: Halsbury's Laws of England, 4th edition, Volume 9(2), page 521.

- fearlessly

investigated.[56]

A Coroner can play an active and pro-active role in the investigation process.[57]

The Coroner has very wide powers to direct any person to do anything that will assist the investigation.[58]

This can include directions to police officers[59] or expert witnesses[60] to:

- take photographs;
- prepare maps, plans and reports;
- obtain documents, such as statements and addendum statements that are more detailed;

  and

- collect evidence, such as a weapon or bullet.[61]

---

[56] See *R v Her Majesty's Coroner of North Humberside and Scunthorpe; ex parte Jamieson* [1995] QB 1 at 26, (1994) 158 JP 1011 at 1035.

[57] See section 6 of the *Coroners Act* (Ch. 32).

[58] See section 6 of the *Coroners Act* (Ch. 32).

[59] See *The State v Jacob Toroken, Coroner; ex parte George Nelson Perera* (1981) N281.

[60] Refer also to the section titled 'Opinion Evidence' in the chapter titled 'Evidence' in the text titled 'Injia on Criminal Practice and Procedure in Papua New Guinea and the Pacific'.

[61] See section 6 of the *Coroners Act* (Ch. 32).

INTRODUCTION

Depending on the circumstances a Coroner may call in experts, such as forensic experts, mine inspectors, engineers, fire officers and medical experts, in order to assist in the investigation process.

A visit to the scene of an incident can assist the Coroner to gain a better understanding of the circumstances relevant to the inquest.[62]

Statements, photographs, plans and sketches do not always provide a good description of the scene of an incident.

A Coroner may also call on the assistance of the media in the investigation stage, such as assisting in the identification of witnesses to a particular incident or the body of a deceased.

Although the investigation and coronial inquest are under the complete direction and control of the Coroner, an interested party or their legal representative may attempt to interfere with the investigation or inquest.

However, the Coroner is in absolute control.

It is ultimately the responsibility of the Coroner to ensure that each facet of the coronial process operates effectively.[63]

The Coroner must set the bounds of the coronial inquest and he or she must rule on the procedure to be followed.[64]

---

[62] As regards viewing the body of a deceased, see section 12 of the *Coroners Act* (Ch. 32).

[63] See New Zealand Law Commission, 2000, 'Coroners', Report 62, page 75.

[64] See Halsbury's Laws of England, 4th edition, Volume 9(2), page 521.

INTRODUCTION

At a coronial inquest a Coroner:

- has to make a finding[65];
- may make comments;

  and

- may make a recommendation.

Such findings, comments and recommendations must however be based on the evidence.

The decisions of a Coroner, like those of any other judicial officer, must be respected unless and until they are varied or overruled.[66]

A Coroner, like any other judicial officer, is immune from legal proceedings in respect to words spoken or acts done in the course of his or her duty[67], provided he or she is acting within his or her jurisdiction, power and authority[68].

Whenever an expatriate dies or is reported missing and that expatriate is not a permanent resident of Papua New Guinea then the relevant consulate should be advised.

---

[65] See *Musumeci v Attorney-General of New South Wales and another* (2003) 57 NSWLR 193, [2003] NSWCA 77.

[66] See *R v Her Majesty's Coroner of North Humberside and Scunthorpe; ex parte Jamieson* [1995] QB 1 at 26, (1994) 158 JP 1011 and *The Queen on the Application of the Commissioner of Police for the Metropolis v Her Majesty's Coroner for Southern District of Greater London* [2003] EWHC Admin 1829.

See also: Halsbury's Laws of England, 4th edition, Volume 9(2), page 521.

[67] See *Everett v Griffiths* [1921] AC 631.

[68] See *Foxhall v Barnett* (1853) 2 E & B 928.

APPOINTMENT OF A CORONER

Section 2 of the *Coroners Act* (Ch. 32) states:

'(1) The Judicial and Legal Services Commission may, by notice in the National Gazette –

(a) appoint a person[69] to be a Coroner; and

(b) specify the province or provinces within which he has jurisdiction, power and authority as a Coroner.[70]

(2) A Coroner appointed under Subsection (1) may hold a coronial inquest in connection with a death or a fire that occurs, or on a dead body that is found, only within the province or provinces within which he has jurisdiction, power and authority as a Coroner'.

Section 3 states:

'District Officers[71] are, by virtue of their offices, Coroners and have jurisdiction, power and authority as Coroners throughout the country'.

---

[69] Whilst a Coroner is not required to be legally or medically qualified [see *Re Sutherland* [1994] 2 NZLR 242, per Barker ACJ] in some instances, a Coroner who is not legally trained may have difficulty understanding the scope of their role [see *R v Her Majesty's Coroner for Inner North London District; ex parte Linnane* (1990) 155 JP 343, [1989] 2 All ER 254, [1989] 1 WLR 395].

[70] As to whether there is the need for a Chief Coroner, see New Zealand Law Commission, 1999, 'Coroner A Review A Discussion Paper', Preliminary Paper 36, page 21 and New Zealand Law Commission, 2000, 'Coroners', Report 62, page 24.

[71] Section 3(1) of the *Interpretation Act* (Ch. 2) defines the term 'District Officer' as including a person occupying one of the following offices:

- District Officer;
- Assistant District Officer;
- Patrol Officer; and
- Assistant Patrol Officer.

APPOINTMENT OF A CORONER

Section 4 states:

> 'A Coroner who is a medical practitioner is not competent or compellable to hold a coronial inquest on the body of a person whom he attended professionally at or immediately before his death or during his last illness'.

DEATH INQUEST

[1.0] INTRODUCTION

The holding of a coronial inquest into the death of a person by a Coroner has a long tradition, when account is taken of its English roots.[72]

It is a fact-finding inquiry conducted by the Coroner to ascertain the facts or matters relating to the death required by the relevant statutory provisions.[73]

A coronial inquest into the death of a person invariably involves the public interest.[74]

Whilst the State has an interest in ascertaining, as precisely as possible, the cause of all deaths the underlying objectives are:

- to identify dangerous or negligent practices that have cost human lives;

  and then

- to modify or eliminate them.[75]

---

[72] See *R v North Humberside and Scunthorpe Coroner; ex parte Jamieson* [1995] QB 1 at 11, (1994) 158 JP 1011.

See also: *Atkinson v Morrow and another* [2005] QSC 92.

[73] See *R v North Humberside and Scunthorpe Coroner; ex parte Jamieson* [1995] QB 1 at 23, (1994) 158 JP 1011.

See also: *Atkinson v Morrow and another* [2005] QSC 92.

[74] See *R v North Humberside and Scunthorpe Coroner; ex parte Jamieson* [1995] QB 1 at 23, (1994) 158 JP 1011; *Annetts v McCann* (1990) 170 CLR 596 at 603, [1990] HCA 57; *Atkinson v Morrow and another* [2005] QSC 92 and *R v South London Coroner; ex parte Thompson* (1982) 126 Sol Jo 625.

[75] See New Zealand Law Commission, 1999, 'Coroner A Review A Discussion Paper', Preliminary Paper 36, page 1 and New Zealand Law Commission, 2000, 'Coroners', Report 62, page 1.

DEATH INQUEST

The function of a coronial inquest into the death of a person is to seek out and record as many of the facts concerning the death as the public interest requires[76], including:

- establishing whether a person has in fact died[77];

- establishing their identity[78];

- establishing when and where they died[79];

- determining the entire circumstances of the death[80];

  and

- establishing the 'manner' and 'medical cause' of their death.[81]

In making a determination as to the 'manner' and 'medical cause' of a death a coronial inquest is not limited to those facts that are immediately proximate to the time of the death of the deceased.[82]

---

[76] See *R v South London Coroner; ex parte Thompson* (1982) 126 SJ 625, per Lane LCJ.

[77] See New Zealand Law Commission, 2000, 'Coroners', Report 62, page 3.

[78] See New Zealand Law Commission, 2000, 'Coroners', Report 62, page 3.

[79] See New Zealand Law Commission, 2000, 'Coroners', Report 62, page 3.

[80] See *Sakawan Kasieng v Andrew Baigry, Magistrate of Wewak District Court and The State* (2004) N2562.

[81] See New Zealand Law Commission, 2000, 'Coroners', Report 62, page 3.

[82] See *WRB Transport and others v Chivell* [1998] SASC 7002.

If in the opinion of the Coroner the death appears to have been unnatural or violent, the Coroner must consider whether this appears to have been due to the actions or inaction of any person.[83]

The Coroner is ultimately responsible for ensuring that each facet of the coronial process operates effectively, including ensuring that there is ongoing and comprehensive communication with the family of the deceased.[84]

[2.0] JURISDICTION

Section 7 of the *Coroners Act* (Ch. 32) provides that a Coroner has the jurisdiction to inquire into the 'manner'[85] and 'cause'[86] of the death of a person who:

- was killed;
- drowned;
- died under suspicious or unusual circumstances;
- died under an anesthetic in the course of a medical, surgical or dental operation or an operation of a like nature;

83 See New Zealand Law Commission, 2000, 'Coroners', Report 62, page 3.

84 See New Zealand Law Commission, 2000, 'Coroners', Report 62, page 75.

85 The 'manner' relates to the circumstances that resulted in the 'medical cause' of death.

86 The 'cause' relates to the 'medical' cause of death.

- died a sudden death of which the cause is unknown[87];

- died, but no certificate of a medical practitioner has been given as to the cause of death;

- died within a year and a day after the date of an accident where the cause of death is directly attributable to the accident[88];

- died in a corrective institution, rural lock-up or police lock-up, or while a prisoner or in custody;

- died in a mental hospital or other institution under such circumstances as to require a coronial inquest under the *Coroners Act* (Ch. 32) or any other enactment;

- died in such circumstances that, in the opinion of the Attorney-General, the cause of death and the circumstances of the death should be more clearly and definitely ascertained;

  or

- died, not having been attended by a medical practitioner at any time within three months before his or her death.

---

87 The expression 'cause of death is unknown' means either that the terminal cause of death is not known or that the terminal cause of death is known, but not the underlying condition which is the real cause of death, see *R v Her Majesty's Coroner for South District of Greater London; ex parte Valarie Patricia Weeks* [1996] EWHC Admin 329.

An unexpected death is usually construed as a sudden death of which the cause is unknown, see Halsbury's Laws of England, 4th edition, Volume 9(2), page 494.

88 The ordinary meaning of the term 'misadventure' is no different to 'accident', see *R v Portsmouth Coroner; ex parte Anderson* [1987] 1 WLR 1640, per Mann J at 1644-1646.

DEATH INQUEST

A Coroner shall inquire without delay into the manner and cause of a death as specified in section 7(1) of the *Coroners Act* (Ch. 32)[89]:

- prior to the expiration of 12 months from the date of a death;

- prior to the expiration of 12 months from the date of finding a dead body (whichever is the later),

  or

- unless otherwise directed by the Attorney-General.[90]

A failure to comply with the provisions of section 7(3) of the *Coroners Act* (Ch. 32) will result in a Coroners Court acting outside of its jurisdiction.[91]

[3.0] NO INQUEST

A Coroner may exercise his or her discretion not to hold a coronial inquest into a death if he or she considers that no good purpose would be served by the holding of such an inquest[92] from the point of view of society[93], unless:

- directed by the Attorney-General[94];

---

[89] See section 7(2) of the *Coroners Act* (Ch. 32).

[90] See section 7(3) of the *Coroners Act* (Ch. 32).

[91] See *Sakawar Kasieng v Andrew Baigry, Magistrate of Wewak District Court and The State* (2004) N2562.

[92] See section 7(4) of the *Coroners Act* (Ch. 32).

[93] See *The State v Jacob Toroken, Coroner; ex parte George Nelson Perera* (1981) N281.

[94] See section 7(3) of the *Coroners Act* (Ch. 32).

or

- otherwise required by law to hold a coronial inquest[95].

The test to be applied by a Coroner in determining whether to hold a coronial inquest into a death is one of 'objective fact'.[96]

The matters that are to be considered are not limited to admissible evidence.[97]

If a sudden death is reported then a coronial inquest should be held, unless there is credible information as may be sufficient to satisfy a reasonable mind that the death was due to a natural cause.[98]

The Coroner must ensure that the relevant facts are exposed to public scrutiny, particularly if there is evidence of:

- foul play;

- abuse;

or

- inhumanity.[99]

---

[95] See section 7(6) of the *Coroners Act* (Ch. 32).

[96] See *R v Her Majesty's Coroner for South District of Greater London; ex parte Valerie Patricia Weeks* [1996] EWHC Admin 329.

[97] See *Hussein v Chung Fook Kam* [1970] AC 942 at 949.

[98] See *Re Hall* (1882) 9 QBD 689, per Lord Selborne at 700.

[99] See Halsbury's Laws of England, 4th edition, Volume 9(2), page 521.

DEATH INQUEST

It may be advisable for a Coroner to consult the next of kin of the deceased and other interested parties in order to determine whether it is necessary to hold a coronial inquest.

If a Coroner does not hold a coronial inquest he or she is required to forward to the Attorney-General the following documentation:

- a certificate in the prescribed form referred to as the 'Coroner's Certificate Where No Inquest On Death Will Serve No Good Purpose' stating the reason for coming to that decision and showing particulars of the deceased and the cause of his or her death[100];

- a copy of any medical certificate or 'Post-Mortem Examination Report' made in connection with the death;

- copies of all other reports that have come to his or her attention dealing with the death where any of the information acted on by the Coroner is information that he or she obtained otherwise than from reports;

  and

- a copy of his or her own report on the death.[101]

The Coroner should notify the next of kin of the deceased and any interested parties of any such decision, particularly where there have been allegations of foul play or other suspicious circumstances, such as suspected poisoning, unlawful assault or sorcery.

---

[100] See section 1(k) and Form 11 of the *Coroners Regulation* (Ch. 32).

A copy of that certificate is also to be sent to the Commissioner of Police, see section 7(5) of the *Coroners Act* (Ch. 32).

[101] See section 7(4) of the *Coroners Act* (Ch. 32).

However, where the Attorney-General directs a Coroner to hold a coronial inquest, he or she shall hold the inquest.[102]

Whether or not a coronial inquest is held the Coroner is required to forward to the Registrar-General notice in the prescribed form[103] of the death.[104]

Where, after considering any information as to the death of a person as specified in section 7(1) of the *Coroners Act* (Ch. 32), a Coroner is satisfied that a medical practitioner knows the immediate cause of death, whether as the result of a post-mortem examination or otherwise, he or she may consent to that medical practitioner forwarding a medical certificate or post-mortem certificate of the cause of death to the Registrar-General.[105]

[4.0] INITIAL REPORT

Where:

- a dead body is found;

  or

- in a case of sudden death or death attended with suspicious or unusual circumstances occurs,

[102] See section 21(1)(b) of the *Coroners Act* (Ch. 32).

[103] There is however no prescribed form in the *Coroners Act* (Ch. 32) or the *Coroners Regulation* (Ch. 32).

[104] See section 8(1) of the *Coroners Act* (Ch. 32).

[105] See section 8(2) of the *Coroners Act* (Ch. 32).

a person:

- knowing;

  or

- becoming acquainted with,

the death or the finding of the body must immediately give notice to the nearest Coroner or a police officer of the rank of Inspector or above.[106]

A person who fails to give such a notice commits an offence.[107]

A police officer who receives notice or otherwise becomes aware of:

- a death as specified in section 7(1) of the *Coroners Act* (Ch. 32);

  or

- a dead body being found,

must without delay give to a Coroner such information as that officer can obtain concerning the death or the dead body.[108]

The police officer is to complete an 'Initial Report Of Death To Coroner' form.[109]

---

106 See section 9(1) of the *Coroners Act* (Ch. 32).

107 See section 9(1) of the *Coroners Act* (Ch. 32).

108 See section 9(2) of the *Coroners Act* (Ch. 32).

109 See Appendix 1.

DEATH INQUEST

When a police officer is advised of a death that officer is to obtain the following information:

- the full name, address and mobile telephone number of the person reporting the death;
- the identity of the deceased, if known;
- the location of the last residence of the deceased, if known;
- the location of the body of the deceased;

  and

- the circumstances of the death.

When a death is reported to a Coroner, he or she should:

- ensure that the relevant entries are made in the court register;
- ensure that a court file is opened and the cover sheet is regularly updated;

  and

- ensure that an 'Initial Report Of Death To Coroner' form[110] has been completed.

Upon a death being reported to the Coroner the body of the deceased is under the control of the Coroner.

[110] See Appendix 1.

DEATH INQUEST

[5.0] VIEW

Whilst a coronial inquest is required to be held as soon as practicable after receiving information in relation to the death of a person as specified in section 7(1) of the *Coroners Act* (Ch. 32)[111], it is not necessary for a Coroner to view the body of a deceased, unless the Coroner thinks that it is advisable to do so[112].

[6.0] NON-SUSPICIOUS AND NON-UNUSUAL DEATH

A non-suspicious and non-unusual death, includes:

- a suicide;

  and

- a death by misadventure.

If, however, there is any doubt as to whether a death was suspicious or unusual then the death is to be treated as suspicious.

What may appear to be a natural death, without suspicious circumstances, may later prove to be a homicide[113].

---

[111] See section 8(1) of the *Coroners Act* (Ch. 32).

[112] See section 12 of the *Coroners Act* (Ch. 32).

[113] Refer also to the section titled 'Homicide Offences' in the chapter titled 'Offences Against The Person' in the text titled 'Injia on Criminal Offences in Papua New Guinea and the Pacific'.

Where there are no suspicious circumstances an investigating officer should attempt to ascertain whether:

- the deceased had attended a medical practitioner, health extension officer or nurse within the previous three months;

  and

- that medical practitioner, health extension officer or nurse will certify the 'medical cause' of death.

Where a medical practitioner, health extension officer or nurse[114] is prepared to give a 'medical cause' of death certificate, but has not attended the deceased within the previous three months, the particulars of the death together with the opinion of the medical practitioner, health extension officer or nurse[115] are to be forwarded to the Coroner by the investigating officer.

If the Coroner does not accept the opinion of the medical practitioner, health extension officer or nurse then a post-mortem examination will need to be performed.

[7.0] INVESTIGATION

The Coroner may play an active and pro-active role in the investigation process and therefore, may give directions as to how an investigation is to be conducted.[116]

---

[114] Refer also to the section titled 'Medical Evidence' in the chapter titled 'Evidence' in the text titled 'Injia on Criminal Practice and Procedure in Papua New Guinea and the Pacific'.

[115] The law in relation to opinion evidence is examined in the section titled 'Opinion Evidence' in the chapter titled 'Evidence' in the text titled 'Injia on Criminal Practice and Procedure in Papua New Guinea and the Pacific'.

[116] See sections 6 and 10(a) of the *Coroners Act* (Ch. 32).

DEATH INQUEST

A deceased must be positively identified.

If the deceased has been identified by a member of his or her immediate family then the nearest relative of adult age must be advised personally.

Irrespective, communication with the family of a deceased is to be conducted in a respectful and sympathetic manner.

The location in the immediate vicinity of a deceased is to be treated as a 'crime scene'[117], until it is established to the satisfaction of the Coroner that no criminal offence has been committed.

The body of a deceased should be covered if found exposed to the public view.

The position of the body of a deceased should be carefully recorded before it is moved.

If possible, it should be photographed in situ.

The body of a deceased should be accompanied by a police officer to a mortuary where it should be:

- stripped and searched thoroughly for valuable items;

  and

- inspected closely for any signs of violence.

The clothing worn by the deceased should be taken possession of for possible evidentiary purposes.

---

[117] Refer also to the chapters titled 'Incident Management' and 'Principles Of Investigation' in the text titled 'Injia on Investigatory Practice in Papua New Guinea and the Pacific'.

A post-mortem examination should not be performed, unless otherwise directed by a Coroner.

The Coroner may direct that further investigation be conducted prior to the commencement of a coronial inquest.[118]

[8.0] INVESTIGATION FILE

[8.1] CONTENTS

A comprehensive investigation file should be completed that includes:

- a list of all witnesses from whom there are statements in the file[119];
- a statement under the hand of the investigating officer;
- a statement from the person who identified the body of the deceased and the basis thereof;
- a statement from the police officer to whom the body of the deceased was identified;
- a statement from the person who identified the body of the deceased to the medical practitioner, health extension officer or nurse, if applicable;

---

[118] See section 6 of the *Coroners Act* (Ch. 32).

[119] Considering that the rules of evidence do not strictly apply to a coronial inquest such statements may contain hearsay evidence.

The law in relation to hearsay evidence is examined in the section titled 'Hearsay Evidence' in the chapter titled 'Evidence' in the text titled 'Injia on Criminal Practice and Procedure in Papua New Guinea and the Pacific'.

- a statement from the person/s who located the body of the deceased, including:
  - the date and time that the deceased was located;
  - where the deceased was located;
  - the circumstances of the death;
  - whether in his or her opinion the deceased was dead at the time of being located, and the basis for such an opinion;

    and
  - whether the deceased said anything prior to dying;
- a statement from the person/s who witnessed the death of the deceased, and if no person witnessed the death:
  - the last person who saw the deceased alive;
  - the apparent state of health of the deceased at that time;

    and
  - the behaviour of the deceased at that time;
- a statement from any medical practitioner, health extension officer or nurse who had been treating the deceased immediately prior to his or her death, including:
  - his or her academic qualifications and experience;
  - any medical condition for which the deceased was being treated;

  - the date that the medical practitioner, health extension officer or nurse last saw the deceased and the state of the health of the deceased at that time;

  - details of treatment provided;

  - duration of such treatment;

  - medication prescribed;

  - his or her opinion as to the 'medical cause' of the death of the deceased;

    and

  - whether in his or her opinion there is any need for a post-mortem examination to be performed, and the reasons therefore[120];

- the original statement of the medical practitioner, health extension officer or nurse that specifies:

  - his or her academic qualifications and experience;

  - the date, time and place of the examination of the body of the deceased;

    and

  - that he or she pronounced 'life extinct' and the 'medical cause' of death, if able to do so, after performing such an examination;

[120] Refer also to the section titled 'Medical Evidence' in the chapter titled 'Evidence' in the text titled 'Injia on Criminal Practice and Procedure in Papua New Guinea and the Pacific'.

- a list of all potential exhibits relevant to the investigation;
- the original receipt of any property taken possession of;
- any diagram or plan made in respect of the scene of the death, if considered necessary;
- any photographs taken of the scene of the death;
- any suicide note;
- the original of any Record of Interview conducted and Voluntary Statement obtained;
- the original 'Life Extinct Certificate';
- the original 'Post-Mortem Examination Report';
- a copy of the 'Initial Report Of Death To Coroner' form;

  and

- any other potentially relevant documentary material.

The investigation file should not be released without the approval of the Coroner.

[8.2] COPIES

There needs to be copies made for the following:

- the Coroner;
- the Coroner's Assistant;
- the relatives of the deceased;

  and

- any 'Interested Parties' as approved by the Coroner.

[8.3] INVESTIGATING OFFICER'S STATEMENT

A statement under the hand of the investigating officer should:

- outline the circumstances of the death, including:
  - a summary of the evidence of each witness;

    and

  - a chronological sequence of the steps taken to investigate the 'manner' and 'medical cause' of death of the deceased;
- specify the identity of the deceased;
- specify as how the identity of deceased was confirmed;

- specify the details of the person who identified the deceased;
- specify the details of the investigation conducted;
- specify the details of any suspect or whether any person has been charged in relation to the death of the deceased;
- specify any possible exhibits that have been taken possession of;
- specify the date and time when life was pronounced extinct, and by whom;
- specify the 'medical cause' of death as determined by a medical practitioner, health extension officer or nurse;
- outline his or her opinion as to the 'medical cause' of death of the deceased and the basis thereto, including the injuries observed to have been suffered by the deceased, if any;
- provide a full description of the circumstances and surroundings in which the body of the deceased was viewed;
- provide a detailed description of the position of the body of the deceased;
- specify any associated pertinent details, such as a rifle laying beside the body of the deceased;
- outline whether the deceased was the subject of a Missing Person Report;
- outline whether a Coroner was advised of the death and if so, who and when;

- specify how the body of the deceased was removed from the scene and to where;
- specify the date and location of the burial;
- specify who approved the burial;
- specify the names and addresses of relatives who have been advised of the death of the deceased, and when;
- outline what the photographs that are attached to the statement depict, together with a list of the photographs;
- specify whether a coronial inquest should be held, and the reasons therefore;

  and

- specify whether the relatives of the deceased have requested that a coronial inquest be held, and the reasons therefore.

[9.0] DEATH IN CUSTODY

[9.1] INTRODUCTION

In any case where a death has occurred in custody it is not a minor or unimportant duty.[121]

[121] See *Reeves v Commissioner of Police of the Metropolis* [2000] 1 AC 360.

DEATH INQUEST

A profound respect for the sanctity of human life underpins the common law.[122]

The State is to ensure that life of a person in custody is not unlawfully taken.[123]

There is a great responsibility on the police and prison authorities to ensure that a citizen in its custody is not deprived of his or her right to life.[124]

Whenever a person dies:

- in a correctional institution[125];
- in a rural lock-up[126];
- in a police lock-up[127];
- while a prisoner;

  or

- in custody[128]

---

122 See *R v Secretary of State for the Home Department; ex parte Amin* [2003] 3 WLR 1169, [2004] 1 AC 653, [1998] 1 WLR 972, [2004] UKHRR 75, (2004) 76 BMLR 143, [2003] 4 All ER 1264, [2004] HRLR 3, 15 BHRC 362 [2003] UKHL 51, per Lord Bingham.

123 See *R v Secretary of State for the Home Department; ex parte Amin* [2003] 3 WLR 1169, [2004] 1 AC 653, [1998] 1 WLR 972, [2004] UKHRR 75, (2004) 76 BMLR 143, [2003] 4 All ER 1264, [2004] HRLR 3, 15 BHRC 362 [2003] UKHL 51, per Lord Bingham.

124 See *Nilabati Behera v State of Orissa* (1993) 2 SCC 746, per Anand J at 767.

125 See section 63 of the *Correctional Service Act 1995*.

126 See section 64 of the *Correctional Service Act 1995*.

127 See section 65 of the *Correctional Service Act 1995*.

128 See section 7(1)(h) of the *Coroners Act* (Ch. 32).

a coronial inquest should ordinarily be held.[129]

A person who is transferred from a police station to a hospital remains in police custody, even though he or she is not at the time being held by a specific police officer.[130]

A Coroner must recognise the acute public concern rightly aroused when a death in custody occurs.

The Coroner must ensure that the relevant facts are exposed to public scrutiny, particularly if there is evidence of:

- foul play;
- abuse;

  or

- inhumanity.[131]

[9.2] INVESTIGATION

The duty to investigate is partly one owed to:

- the next of kin of a deceased as representing the deceased;

---

[129] See International Human Rights Instrument titled 'Body of Principals for the Protection of All Persons under Any Form of Detention or Imprisonment' -- Principal 34.

[130] See *R v Her Majesty's Coroner for Inner London North District; ex parte Linnane* [1989] 1 WLR 395 at 399, (1990) 155 JP 343, [1989] 2 All ER 254.

[131] See *Her Majesty's Coroner for North Humberside and Scunthorpe; ex parte Jamieson* [1995] QB 1 at 26, (1994) 158 JP 1011 at 1035.

and

- the other persons who may in similar circumstances be vulnerable and whose lives may need to be protected.[132]

An investigation into a death in custody should be:

- as independent as possible;
- effective;
- reasonably prompt;
- the subject of public scrutiny;

  and

- held with involvement of the next of kin of the deceased to an appropriate extent.[133]

Obviously such an investigation must also be thorough.[134]

The Coroner may need to hold a preliminary inquest and examine specific witnesses in order to determine the 'medical cause' of death.

---

132 See *Menson v United Kingdom* (Unrep. Application No 47916/99, 6 May 2003), per Lord Slynn at 13.

133 See *Jordan v United Kingdom* (2001) 37 EHRR 52 and *R v Secretary of State for the Home Department; ex parte Amin* [2003] 3 WLR 1169, [2004] 1 AC 653, [1998] 1 WLR 972, [2004] UKHRR 75, (2004) 76 BMLR 143, [2003] 4 All ER 1264, [2004] HRLR 3, 15 BHRC 362 [2003] UKHL 51.

134 See *R v Southwark Coroner; ex parte Hicks* [1987] 1 WLR 1624 and *R v Her Majesty's Coroner for Lincolnshire; ex parte Annette Hay (In Re: Brett Andrew Hay deceased)* [1999] EWHC Admin 155.

[9.3] DUTY OF CARE

Section 283 of the *Criminal Code* (Ch. 262) states (in part):

'(1) It is the duty of every person having charge of another who –

(a) is unable by reason of detention to withdraw himself from that charge; and

(b) is unable to provide himself with the necessaries of life, whether the charge –

(d) is imposed by law

to provide for the other person the necessaries of life.

(2) A person on whom a duty is imposed by Subsection (1) shall be deemed to have caused any consequences that result to the life or health of the other person by reason of any omission to perform that duty'.

Whenever a death in custody occurs following a breach of another's duty of care, the death is deemed to be 'unnatural' and the Coroner has a duty to investigate.[135]

Culpable failure of a person owing a duty of care can result in a person being charged with 'Manslaughter[136]' as a consequence of death occurring that was preventable by proper care.[137]

---

[135] See *R v Price* (1884) 12 QBD 247 at 248.

See also: Thurston's Coronership, 3rd edition, 1985, page 82.

[136] See section 302 of the *Criminal Code* (Ch. 262).

The law in relation to the offence of 'Manslaughter' is examined in the section titled 'Homicide Offences' in the chapter titled 'Offences Against The Person' in the text titled 'Injia on Criminal Offences in Papua New Guinea and the Pacific'.

[137] See *R v Surrey Coroner; ex parte Campbell* [1982] QB 661 at 675-676; *R v Her Majesty's Coroner for Inner South London District; ex parte Kendall* [1988] 1 WLR 1186 at 1192-1193 and *Ex parte Hicks* [1987] 1 WLR 1624 at 1632 and 1634.

[9.4] AVOIDABLE HARM

Reasonable care must be taken to safeguard the lives of persons in custody against the risk of avoidable harm.[138]

Persons in custody must also be protected against self-harm.[139]

[9.5] BRUTALITY

Persons in custody must be protected against violence or abuse at the hands of police or prison officers.[140]

[10.0] IDENTIFICATION OF A DECEASED

[10.1] WHO SHOULD IDENTIFY A DECEASED

Before the Coroner is required to determine the name of the deceased it is important that the investigating officer arranges for a relative or close family friend to:

- identify the body of the deceased;

  and

---

[138] See *R v Secretary of State for the Home Department; ex parte Amin* [2003] 3 WLR 1169, [2004] 1 AC 653, [1998] 1 WLR 972, [2004] UKHRR 75, (2004) 76 BMLR 143, [2003] 4 All ER 1264, [2004] HRLR 3, 15 BHRC 362 [2003] UKHL 51, per Lord Bingham.

[139] See *Reeves v Commissioner of Police of the Metropolis* [2000] 1 AC 360.

[140] See *R v Secretary of State for the Home Department; ex parte Amin* [2003] 3 WLR 1169, [2004] 1 AC 653, [1998] 1 WLR 972, [2004] UKHRR 75, (2004) 76 BMLR 143, [2003] 4 All ER 1264, [2004] HRLR 3, 15 BHRC 362 [2003] UKHL 51, per Lord Bingham.

- make a formal statement of identification.

Friends or work colleagues who have known the deceased for a reasonable period of time, preferably at least 12 months, are also acceptable.

The person identifying the deceased should, where possible, view the body directly.

A statement from a person identifying the body of a deceased must include:

- their full and correct name, address and date and place of birth;
- the witness's relationship to the deceased;

  and

- the duration of the friendship, if a relative cannot identify the body of the deceased.

It is of particular importance to ensure that the full name of a deceased is spelt correctly.

[10.2] METHODS OF IDENTIFICATION

[10.2.1] INTRODUCTION

A simple visual identification will not be possible where:

- a body of a deceased cannot be recognised;

  or

- the identity of the body of the deceased is unknown,

In such circumstances other means of identification will need to be adopted in order to establish the identity of the body of the deceased.

If the identification of a deceased is difficult to determine then the Coroner should be advised.

A coronial inquest must be held when a body of a deceased cannot be identified.[141]

[10.2.2] FINGERPRINTS

A comparison of the fingerprints of the deceased with those on file at the Criminal Records Office may be used to identify the body of a deceased.

[10.2.3] DENTAL RECORDS

The jaw/dentures of a deceased are removed and compared with dental records in order to identify the deceased.

[10.2.4] DISTINCTIVE MARKINGS

The body of a deceased may be identified by means of tattoos, birthmarks and other body marks, such as scars.

[141] See section 7(1)(c) and (d) of the *Coroners Act* (Ch. 32).

[10.2.5] PERSONAL PROPERTY

Depending on the circumstances, the body of a deceased may be identified if the deceased was wearing distinctive jewellery, clothing and other personal property at the time of his or her death.

[10.2.6] DNA TEST

Saliva is an excellent source of DNA.

DNA stands for deoxyribonucleic acid and is found in most of the body's cells.

The probability of two people having the same DNA profile is statistically almost incomprehensible.

Extraction of DNA from blood or other bodily tissue is a very complex process and can be very expensive.

However, DNA analysis is currently not yet available in Papua New Guinea.

Any inquiries for such testing should be made through the National Forensic Science Centre.

[10.2.7] X-RAYS

A comparison of x-rays of old limb fractures, plates, prostheses, etc., may be made with medical records.

[10.2.8] PERSONAL IDENTIFICATION DOCUMENTATION

A comparison may be made with the passport or any other piece of identification that has the particulars of the deceased and his or her photograph.

[11.0] POST-MORTEM EXAMINATION

The Coroner has the power to order whether a post-mortem examination, as referred to as an 'autopsy', should be performed at any time before the termination of a coronial inquest[142], with or without an analysis of the contents of the stomach, intestines or other organs.[143]

The Coroner may order an exhumation, if necessary.[144]

However, a Coroner has no authority to order the removal of the body of a deceased from a morgue without a sufficient lawful reason.[145]

An investigating officer should:

- seek the authority of the Coroner for a post-mortem examination to be performed in order to ascertain the 'medical cause' of death, if necessary;
- advise the pathologist performing the post-mortem examination as to the identification of the deceased;

---

142 See *R v Bristol Coroner; ex parte Kerr* [1974] 1 QB 652 at 658-659, [1974] 2 All ER 719.

143 See section 14(1) of the *Coroners Act* (Ch. 32).

144 See section 11 of the *Coroners Act* (Ch. 32).

145 See *Nells Aingiris for himself and on behalf of 14 others v Orim Karapo and The State* (2008) N3325.

and

- remain during the course of the examination.

Ideally a post-mortem examination should be performed within 24 hours of death.

The exercise of the discretion as to whether a post-mortem examination should be performed is one that is not fettered in any way.[146]

Each decision whether to conduct a post-mortem examination must:

- be determined in light of its own facts and circumstances;

  and

- involve a careful and sensitive consideration of all of the relevant facts and circumstances.[147]

In determining whether to order a post-mortem examination there a number of competing interests, including:

- whether it appears to the Coroner that the 'medical cause' of death of the deceased has not been satisfactorily explained by the evidence of the medical practitioner, health extension officer, nurse or other witnesses[148];

---

146 See *Wuridjal v The Coroner* [2001] NTSC 99.

147 See *Re Death of Simon Unchango (Jnr); ex parte Simon Unchango (Snr)* (1997) 95 A Crim R 65.

148 See section 14(3) of the *Coroners Act* (Ch. 32).

See also: *Krantz v Hand* [1999] NSWSC 432.

See also: New Zealand Law Commission, 1999, 'Coroner A Review A Discussion Paper', Preliminary Paper 36, page 1 and New Zealand Law Commission, 1999, 'Coroner A Review A Discussion Paper', Preliminary Paper 36, page 3.

- whether it appears to the Coroner that the 'medical cause' of death of the deceased was or might have been caused partly or wholly by improper treatment by a medical practitioner, health extension officer, nurse or other person[149];

- when a medical practitioner, health extension officer or nurse is unable to issue a certificate as to the 'medical cause' of death of a deceased;

- when a medical certificate has been issued, but the Coroner is not satisfied as to the nominated 'medical cause' of death of a deceased;

- whether the 'medical cause' of death of a deceased is unknown[150];

- whether the 'medical cause' of death of a deceased is in doubt[151];

- when there is a doubt as to whether the deceased was a still-born child[152];

  and

- the wishes of the family, relatives and friends of the deceased generally based upon cultural or religious beliefs that are genuinely and strongly held.[153]

---

149 See section 14(2) of the *Coroners Act* (Ch. 32).

150 See section 14(4) of the *Coroners Act* (Ch. 32).

151 See section 14(4) of the *Coroners Act* (Ch. 32).

152 See section 14(4) of the *Coroners Act* (Ch. 32).

153 See *Wuridjal v The Coroner* [2001] NTSC 99; *Green v Johnstone* [1995] 2 VR 176, per Beach J at 179; *Ronan v The State Coroner* [2000] WASC 260; *Saunders v State Coroner of Victoria* [2005] VSC 460 and *Re Death of Simon Unchango (Jnr); ex parte Simon Unchango (Snr)* (1997) 95 A Crim R 65, per Walsh J at 70.

See also: New Zealand Law Commission, 1999, 'Coroner A Review A Discussion Paper', Preliminary Paper 36, page 1 and New Zealand Law Commission, 1999, 'Coroner A Review A Discussion Paper', Preliminary Paper 36, page 3.

> People have differing views and practices regarding death based on their culture and religion.[154]
>
> The wishes of the family, relatives and friends of a deceased must however be balanced against the interests of the community that the 'medical cause' and manner of an otherwise unexplained death be ascertained, if possible.[155]

If only marginal assistance will be provided by performing a post-mortem examination then a Coroner may give more weight to that fact.[156]

Whilst the result of a post-mortem examination will assist the Coroner to establish the 'medical cause' of death, it will not necessarily establish what occurred that resulted in that cause of death, ie., the 'manner' of death.

A Coroner should work closely with pathologists and medical practitioners in order to ensure that a post-mortem examination is performed promptly and reported in a timely manner.

Delays can lead to problems later with:

- witnesses being difficult to locate;
- the body of the deceased being buried;
- evidence being destroyed, lost or removed;

---

[154] See New Zealand Law Commission, 1999, 'Coroner A Review A Discussion Paper', Preliminary Paper 36, page 8.

[155] See *Green v Johnstone* [1995] 2 VR 176 at 178.

[156] See *Abernethy v Deitz* (1996) 39 NSWLR 701 at 708.

and

- various other unforeseen problems.

A pathologist may merely hold a visual inspection of the body of a deceased in order to establish a 'medical cause' of death.

However, it is more common for a full post-mortem examination to be carried out.

This will mean that the body of a deceased will be dissected in order to find a primary, and sometimes secondary 'medical cause' of death.

A post-mortem examination will usually involve examining certain organs, bones and tissue by the opening of the skull, chest cage and stomach cavities.

Sometimes other more specific and detailed tests may need to be carried out, such as:

- histology (taking samples of tissue for further microscopic examination);

  and

- toxicology (taking fluid and other samples from the stomach or blood for testing, usually for poisons or other foreign substances).

Such tests may take weeks and even months in order to be completed.

However, where it appears to the Coroner that the death of a deceased was or might have been caused partly or wholly by improper treatment by a medical practitioner or other person, the medical practitioner or other person must not be allowed to perform or assist at the post-mortem examination.[157]

[157] See section 14(2) of the *Coroners Act* (Ch. 32).

DEATH INQUEST

When a medical practitioner not in the Public Service who performs a post-mortem examination of the body of a deceased at the direction of the Coroner, he or she is entitled to be paid such sum as is prescribed for the post-mortem examination[158] upon production of the certificate[159] to the Attorney-General's department.

Upon a post-mortem examination being performed:

- the pathologist should issue a 'Post-Mortem Examination Report', the original of which should be attached to the investigation file;

  and

- the investigating officer should take possession of the clothing of the deceased if it is of any evidentiary value.

Upon completion of a post-mortem examination the investigating officer is responsible for the delivery of the 'Post-Mortem Examination Report' to the Coroner.

---

[158] See section 31(2) of the *Coroners Act* (Ch. 32).

See also: section 2 of the *Coroners Regulation* (Ch. 32).

[159] See section 31(1) of the *Coroners Act* (Ch. 32).

There is however no form in the *Coroners Regulation* (Ch. 32).

[12.0] BURIAL

Only the Coroner can release the body of the deceased for burial[160].

Those persons responsible for the estate of a deceased have a duty to see to a proper burial according to law.[161]

The right to receive a body for burial lies with the executor of the will of the deceased or, if there be no will, by those in order of precedence entitled to letters of administration.[162]

This, however, is not an inflexible rule so that this order of precedence will yield to the circumstances of the case.[163]

An executor has the right to a body of a deceased for burial purposes, even against the wishes of the widow.[164]

---

160 See section 1(1) and Form 9 of the *Coroners Regulation* (Ch. 32).

However, there is no reference to that form in the *Coroners Act* (Ch. 32) and there is no provision in that Act in relation to the 'Warrant To Bury'.

161 See *R v Sharpe* (1857) D & B160, 169 ER 959.

162 See *Williams v Williams* (1882) 20 Ch D 659 at 665.

See also: *Murdoch v Rhind and Murdoch* [1945] NZLR 425 at 426-427; *Re Clarke (Deceased)* [1965] NZLR 182 at 183 and *Awa v Independent News (Auckland) Limited* [1995] 3 NZLR 701.

163 See *Leeburn v Derndorfer* (2004) 14 VR 100 at 104, [2004] VSC 172; *Dow v Hoskins* [2003] VSC 206 at 37; *Jones v Dodd* (1999) 73 SASR 328, [1999] SASC 125; *Smith v Tamworth City Council* (1997) 41 NSWLR 680 at 693-694 and *Burnes v Richards* (1993) 7 BPR 15104.

164 See *Hunter v Hunter* (1930) 65 OLR 586.

[12.0] EXHUMATION[165]

When it appears to the Coroner that there is grave suspicion as to the 'medical cause' of the death of a person whose body has been buried, the Coroner may issue his or her warrant[166] for the exhumation of the body for the purpose of holding a coronial inquest.[167]

At common law the National Court may also order the exhumation of the body of a deceased.[168]

Whilst an interested party may make an application to the National Court to prevent an exhumation being conducted, such an application should only be successful if it is shown that the Coroner either:

- was not acting in good faith

  or

- did not have sufficient reasonable grounds to exhume the body.

---

[165] See section 29 of the *Cemeteries Act* (Ch. 302).

[166] See section 1(j) and Form 10 of the *Coroners Regulation* (Ch. 32).

[167] See section 11 of the *Coroners Act* (Ch. 32).

See also: *R v Bristol Coroner; ex parte Kerr* [1974] 1 QB 652, [1974] 2 All ER 719; *Tasmanian Aboriginal Centre Inc, Tasmanian Aboriginal Land Council Aboriginal Corporation and Lehmann, Gregory Patrick v Wilson* [1994] TASSC 65 and *Haydon v Chivell* [1999] SASC 315.

[168] See *Scott and another v Northern Territory of Australia and others* [2005] NTCA 1.

Furthermore, section 16 of the *Coroners Act* (Ch. 32) provides:

- that notwithstanding any law or custom to the contrary it is not lawful for a Coroner to forbid the rites of Christian burial at the interment of a person who has committed suicide or died by his or her own act, nor does a forfeiture or escheat to the State of real or personal property belonging to that person take place by reason of a verdict that he or she committed suicide or died by his or her own act;

  and

- that the verdict of *felo de se*[169], ie., suicide, is abolished.

[169] In early English common law, an adult who committed suicide was literally a felon, and the crime was punishable by forfeiture of property to the King and what was considered a shameful burial – typically with a stake through their heart and with a burial at a crossroad, see Macdonald, M., The Secularization of Suicide in England, 1660-1800, *Past and Present* #111, (May, 1986), pp. 50-100.

FIRE INQUEST

[1.0] INTRODUCTION

A Coroner shall inquire into the 'cause' and 'origin' of a fire by which any property[170] was destroyed or damaged where:

- the Attorney-General directs the Coroner to hold a coronial inquest[171];
- it is requested by a person on:
    - payment by him or her to the Coroner of the sum of K20 or such sum as is prescribed;

      and

    - giving an undertaking to pay any further costs entailed in the holding of the coronial inquest[172].

      The amount of the costs payable is as certified by the Coroner holding the coronial inquest, and may be recovered by the State as a debt.[173]

---

[170] The term 'property' is not defined in either the *Coroners Act* (Ch. 32) or the *Interpretation Act* (Ch. 2).

The plain and ordinary meaning of that term in the context of this section would include anything that is capable of being owned, see The Concise Oxford Dictionary, 5th edition.

Whilst that term is defined in section 1(1) of the *Criminal Code* (Ch. 262) that definition only applies to that Code and is not read either expressly or impliedly 'in pari materia' with the *Coroners Act* (Ch. 32), see section 2 of the *Criminal Code Act* (Ch. 262).

As regards the law in relation to 'Acts in pari materia', refer to the section titled 'Extrinsic Aids' in the chapter titled 'Aids To Interpretation' in the text titled 'Injia on Statutory Interpretation in Papua New Guinea and the Pacific'.

[171] See section 17(1)(b) of the *Coroners Act* (Ch. 32).

[172] See section 18(1) of the *Coroners Act* (Ch. 32).

[173] See section 18(2) of the *Coroners Act* (Ch. 32).

Considering that there is currently no form for this certification, a Coroner may use an official letterhead;

or

- he or she is of the opinion that such a coronial inquest ought to be held.[174]

If the Coroner considers that no good purpose would be served by holding a coronial inquest, he or she shall forward to the Attorney-General:

- a certificate in the prescribed form[175] stating the reason for coming to that decision;
- copies of all other reports that have come to his or her attention dealing with the fire;

  and

- where any of the information acted on by him or her is information that he or she has obtained otherwise than from reports, a copy of his or her own report on the fire.[176]

The range of matters that fall within such a coronial inquest, whilst not open-ended, are those that could be considered relevant to determining the:

- 'cause';

  and

[174] See section 17(1)(a) of the *Coroners Act* (Ch. 32).

[175] See section 1(l) and Form 12 of the *Coroners Regulation* (Ch. 32).

[176] See section 17(2) of the *Coroners Act* (Ch. 32).

- 'origin'

of the fire.[177]

The Coroner must determine:

- what occurred at the 'origin' of the fire, ie., at its beginning which means its starting-point;

  and

- the 'cause' of the fire, ie., the agency or phenomenon that started it.[178]

All intervening or contributing events may be considered.[179]

Clearly that includes the progress of the fire and necessarily involves the efforts, if any, to suppress the fire.[180]

The limiting factor is that of relevance to the issue of 'cause' and 'origin' of the fire process and progress.[181]

---

177 See *R v Doogan; ex parte Lucas-Smith and others* (2006) 158 ACTR 1, [2005] ACTSC 74; sub nom *Re Doogan; ex parte Lucas-Smith and others* (2005) 193 FLR 239, [2005] ACTSC 74.

178 See *R v Doogan; ex parte Lucas-Smith and others* (2006) 158 ACTR 1, [2005] ACTSC 74; sub nom *Re Doogan; ex parte Lucas-Smith and others* (2005) 193 FLR 239, [2005] ACTSC 74.

See also: *Queensland Fire and Rescue Authority v Hall* [1997] QSC 221.

179 See *R v Doogan; ex parte Lucas-Smith and others* (2006) 158 ACTR 1, [2005] ACTSC 74; sub nom *Re Doogan; ex parte Lucas-Smith and others* (2005) 193 FLR 239, [2005] ACTSC 74.

180 See *Lucas-Smith and others v Coroner's Court of the Australian Capital Territory and others* [2009] ACTSC 40.

181 See *Lucas-Smith and others v Coroner's Court of the Australian Capital Territory and others* [2009] ACTSC 40.

It may be necessary for a Coroner to receive evidence in order to determine if it is relevant to or falls in or out of the proper scope of the coronial inquest.[182]

[2.0] INITIAL REPORT

Any fire:

- involving substantial destruction or damage of property;
- that endangered life;

  or

- that is suspicious in nature,

should be reported to a Coroner.

When a police officer is advised of such a fire that officer is to obtain the following information:

- the full name, address and mobile telephone number of the person reporting the fire;
- the location of the fire;
- the cause of the fire, if known;
- what destruction or damage has been caused by the fire;

[182] See *Lucas-Smith and others v Coroner's Court of the Australian Capital Territory and others* [2009] ACTSC 40.

and

- whether any person has been injured or killed as a consequence of the fire.

When a report of a fire is made an 'Initial Report Of Fire To Coroner'[183] form is to be completed.

When a fire is reported to a Coroner, he or she should:

- ensure that the relevant entries are made in the court register;
- ensure that a court file is opened and the cover sheet is regularly updated;

  and

- ensure that an 'Initial Report Of Fire To Coroner' form[184] has been completed.

If there is any doubt as to whether a particular fire should be reported a Coroner is to be contacted.

[3.0] INVESTIGATION

In all circumstances of a fire that should be reported to a Coroner the scene of the fire should be treated as a 'crime scene'[185], until it becomes apparent that no criminal offence has been committed or all forensic evidence has been obtained.

---

[183] See Appendix 2.

[184] See Appendix 2.

[185] Refer also to the chapter titled 'Principles Of Investigation' in the text titled 'Injia on Investigatory Practice in Papua New Guinea and the Pacific'.

FIRE INQUEST

A comprehensive investigation file should be completed and submitted without undue delay to the Coroner in order for the Coroner to determine the 'cause' and 'origin' of the fire.

The Coroner may direct that further investigation be conducted prior to the commencement of a coronial inquest.[186]

[4.0] INVESTIGATION FILE

[4.1] CONTENTS

A comprehensive investigation file should be completed that includes:

- a list of all witnesses from whom there are statements in the file[187];
- a statement under the hand of the investigating officer;
- a statement from the person who located the fire, including:
    - the place where the fire was located;
    - the time that the fire was located;
    - the cause of the fire, if known;

---

[186] See section 17(3) of the *Coroners Act* (Ch. 32).

[187] Considering that the rules of evidence do not strictly apply to a coronial inquest such statements may contain hearsay evidence.

The law in relation to hearsay evidence is examined in the section titled 'Hearsay Evidence' in the chapter titled 'Evidence' in the text titled 'Injia on Criminal Practice and Procedure in Papua New Guinea and the Pacific'.

  - the description and any other particulars of any person seen running away from the vicinity of the scene of the fire, if applicable;

    and

  - the description and any other particulars of any person seen acting suspiciously in the vicinity of the scene of the fire, if applicable;

- a statement from the owner of the property, including:

  - the particulars of the last person to use the property;

  - security procedures installed in relation to the property;

  - the extent of damage or destruction to the property and the estimated value of loss;

  - any insurance details in relation to the property;

    and

  - whether a Fire Inquest is requested to be held and the reasons therefore;

- a statement from the fire officer who is able to give an opinion as to the 'cause' and 'origin' of the fire;

- a statement from a person who has the appropriate forensic qualifications and experience in determining the 'cause' and 'origin' of a fire who is able to give opinion evidence in relation to the fire, if available;

- a list of all potential exhibits;

- a copy of the 'Initial Report Of Fire To Coroner' form;
- any reports from relevant experts;
- any diagram or plan made in respect of the scene of the fire;
- any photographs taken of the scene of the fire;
- the original of any Record of Interview conducted and Voluntary Statement obtained, if applicable;

  and

- any other potentially relevant documentary material.

The investigation file should not be released without the approval of the Coroner.

[4.2] COPIES

There needs to be copies made for the following:

- the Coroner;
- the Coroner's Assistant;
- the owner of the property;

  and

- any 'Interested Parties' as approved by the Coroner.

[4.3] INVESTIGATING OFFICER'S STATEMENT

A statement under the hand of the investigating officer should:

- outline the circumstances of the fire, including:

    - a summary of the evidence of each witness;

      and

    - a chronological sequence of the steps taken to investigate the 'cause' and 'origin' of the fire;

- specify the details of the investigation conducted;

- specify the details of any suspect;

- specify any possible exhibits that have been taken possession of;

  and

- outline what photographs that are attached to the file depict, together with a list of the photographs.

MISSING PERSON INQUEST

[1.0] INTRODUCTION

When:

- a person has been reported to a police officer as missing and the police have not found the missing person within the period of six months after the date of the report;

- a Coroner is of the opinion that a coronial inquest into the disappearance of a missing person ought to be held;

- the Attorney-General directs a Coroner to hold a coronial inquest;

  or

- the Commissioner of Police, a Superintendent of Police or the husband, wife, father, mother, sister, brother, son, daughter or guardian of the missing person requests a Coroner to hold such a coronial inquest[188],

a Coroner shall inquire into:

- the cause and circumstances of the disappearance of the missing person;

  and

- all matters and things

[188] See section 20(6) of the *Coroners Act* (Ch. 32).

that will reveal, or are likely to reveal, whether the missing person is alive or dead, and if the person is alive or likely to be alive his or her whereabouts at the time of the inquiry.[189]

When the disappearance of a missing person is reported to a Coroner, he or she should:

- ensure that the relevant entries are made in the court register;

  and

- ensure that a court file is opened and the cover sheet is regularly updated.

[2.0] INVESTIGATION FILE

[2.1] CONTENTS

An investigation file into the disappearance of a missing person to be forwarded to the Coroner is to include the following documentation:

- a list of all witnesses from whom there are statements in the file[190];

- a statement under the hand of the investigating officer;

- the original statements of all witnesses;

---

[189] See section 20(1) of the *Coroners Act* (Ch. 32).

[190] Considering that the rules of evidence do not strictly apply to a coronial inquest such statements may contain hearsay evidence.

The law in relation to hearsay evidence is examined in the section titled 'Hearsay Evidence' in the chapter titled 'Evidence' in the text titled 'Injia on Criminal Practice and Procedure in Papua New Guinea and the Pacific'.

- a list of all potential exhibits;
- the original of any Record of Interview conducted and Voluntary Statement obtained;

  and
- any other relevant documentation.

The investigation file should not be released without the approval of the Coroner.

[2.2] COPIES

There needs to be copies made for the following:

- the Coroner;
- the Coroner's Assistant;
- the relatives of the missing person;

  and
- any 'Interested Parties' as approved by the Coroner.

[2.3] INVESTIGATING OFFICER'S STATEMENT

A statement under the hand of the investigating officer should:

- specify the particulars of the missing person, including full name, address, age and mobile telephone number;
- outline the circumstances of the disappearance of the missing person, including a summary of the evidence of each witness;
- specify the details of the investigation conducted;
- specify the details of any suspect;
- specify any possible exhibits that have been taken possession of;

  and

- outline what any photographs that are attached to the file depict, together with a list of the photographs.

WITNESS ATTENDANCE

A Coroner may issue a summons in the prescribed form[191] to a person whose evidence he or she thinks it necessary in order to:

- secure his or her attendance at a coronial inquest at the time and place named in the summons;

  and

- give evidence and be examined.[192]

When the Coroner thinks fit on the request of a witness, he or she may grant a certificate to the witness of such amount as the Coroner thinks reasonable for his or her expenses, trouble and loss of time, computed at a rate not exceeding the rate allowed for the attendance of a witness before the National Court in a criminal case.[193]

That certificate has to be produced to the Attorney-General's department for payment.

The term 'trouble' is not defined in either the *Coroners Act* (Ch. 32) or the *Interpretation Act* (Ch. 1).

Therefore, it is at the discretion of the Coroner as to what is the appropriate amount, provided that the amount does not exceed the rate allowed for the attendance of a witness before the National Court in a criminal case.

Legal costs are not regarded as witness expenses.

---

[191] See section 1(a) and Form 1 of the *Coroners Regulation* (Ch. 32).

[192] See section 25(1) of the *Coroners Act* (Ch. 32).

[193] See sections 31(1) and 14(3) of the *Coroners Act* (Ch. 32).

See also: section 2 of the *Coroners Regulation* (Ch. 32).

WITNESS ATTENDANCE

In a coronial inquest concerning the death of a person, a Coroner may summons as a witness:

- a medical practitioner who attended the deceased[194];

  or

- a health extension officer or any other health professional, such as a nurse, who attended the deceased.

A Coroner holding a coronial inquest into the cause and circumstances of the disappearance of a missing person may summons a person to attend the inquest and give evidence.[195]

In a summons or by a written order, the Coroner may require a witness or other person to produce books, documents, writings or any other thing in his or her custody, possession or control that the Coroner thinks ought to be produced.[196]

The Coroner must sign the summons or order issued by him or her.[197]

---

[194] See section 13 of the *Coroners Act* (Ch. 32).

See also: section 1(b) and Form 2 of the *Coroners Regulation* (Ch. 32).

[195] See section 20(2) of the *Coroners Act* (Ch. 32).

[196] See section 25(2) of the *Coroners Act* (Ch. 32).

[197] See section 33 of the *Coroners Act* (Ch. 32).

WITNESS ATTENDANCE

Where a person who has been summonsed to attend as a witness at a coronial inquest:

- fails without reasonable excuse to appear at the inquest[198];

- refuses to take an oath or make an affirmation or be examined at the inquest;

- refuses without reasonable cause to give evidence at the inquest;

  or

- when required by the Coroner, by summons or written order, fails or refuses without reasonable excuse to produce at the inquest books, documents, writings or any other thing in his or her custody, possession or control that the Coroner thinks ought to be produced,

the Coroner may impose a fine not exceeding K40.[199]

When on the appearance of a witness:

- voluntarily;

- in obedience of a summons;

  or

---

198 A Coroner may issue a warrant for the arrest of such a person, see section 28 of the *Coroners Act* (Ch. 32).

See also: section 1(c) and Form 3 of the *Coroners Regulation* (Ch. 32).

199 See section 26(1) of the *Coroners Act* (Ch. 32).

- brought before the Coroner by virtue of a warrant[200]

at a coronial inquest into a missing person the witness:

- refuses without reasonable cause to give evidence at such an inquest;

- refuses without reasonable excuse to take an oath or to make an affirmation or to be examined on oath at such an inquest;

  or

- fails or refuses without reasonable excuse, on being required by the Coroner, to produce at the inquest, books, documents, writings or any other thing in his or her custody, possession or control that the Coroner thinks ought to be produced,

and, at or in respect of the same inquest on a subsequent day, the witness fails or refuses to do any of the things as specified above, the Coroner, irrespective of whether a fine has been imposed for previous failure or refusal, may by his or her warrant commit the witness to a corrective institution or, subject to any other law, to a rural lock-up or police lock-up until the witness consents to be examined and to answer questions concerning the matter, or to produce the books, documents, writings or other thing in question.[201]

---

[200] See section 28 of the *Coroners Act* (Ch. 32).

See also: section 1(c) and Form 3 of the *Coroners Regulation* (Ch. 32).

[201] See sections 26(2) and 28 of the *Coroners Act* (Ch. 32).

COURT PROCEDURE

[1.0] INTRODUCTION

A Coroner is to be treated in the same manner and with the same respect as a Magistrate.

However, at a coronial inquest the Coroner is addressed as 'Sir' or 'Madam', and not 'Your Worship'.

There needs to be a less formal atmosphere than would otherwise be in a court of law in what are usually difficult and emotional circumstances.

It is the duty of the Coroner to:

- set the bounds of the coronial inquest;

  and

- rule on the procedure to be followed.[202]

Such decisions, like that of any other judicial officer, must be respected unless and until such decisions are varied or overruled.[203]

Evidence at a coronial inquest must be recorded.[204]

---

[202] See *R v Her Majesty's Coroner for North Humberside and Scunthorpe; ex parte Jamieson* [1995] QB 1, (1994) 158 JP 1011 at 1035.

[203] See *R v Her Majesty's Coroner for North Humberside and Scunthorpe; ex parte Jamieson* [1995] QB 1, (1994) 158 JP 1011 at 1035.

[204] See section 6 of the *Coroners Act* (Ch. 32).

See also: *Attorney-General v BBC* [1981] AC 303; *R v Surrey Coroner; ex parte Campbell* [1982] QB 661; *X v Deputy State Coroner for New South Wales* (2001) 51 NSWLR 312, [2001] NSWSC 46; *Aplin and another v McIntyre* [2002] QSC 288 and Halsbury's Laws of England, 4th edition, Volume 9(2), page 472.

COURT PROCEDURE

At a coronial inquest a Coroner shall:

- put into writing;

  or

- cause to be put into writing by the Coroner's Clerk

the evidence given before him or her.[205]

In relation to a lengthy or complex coronial inquest it may be necessary to engage the services of a court reporter to record and transcribe the evidence.

It may therefore be advantageous for a Coroner to conduct a pre-hearing conference when there is the potential for a complex or lengthy coronial inquest.

The depositions of a witness taken at a coronial inquest shall be:

- read over to the witness;

  or

- by the witness

and shall be signed by:

- the witness;

  and

---

[205] See section 23(1) of the *Coroners Act* (Ch. 32).

See also: section 1(f) and Form 6 of the *Coroners Regulation* (Ch. 32).

- the Coroner.[206]

At the conclusion of a coronial inquest, and whether a person is committed for trial or not, the Coroner shall:

- forward the depositions to the Attorney-General with his or her findings under sections 10 or 17(4) of the *Coroners Act* (Ch. 32), as the case may be;

  and

- send a duplicate of such findings to the Commissioner of Police and, where the coronial inquest concerns a death, to the Registrar-General.[207]

It is the duty of the Coroner to:

- ensure that the relevant facts are fully, fairly and fearlessly investigated[208];

  and

- confine the legal representative of an interested party to those issues that he or she considers to be relevant.[209]

---

[206] See section 23(2) of the *Coroners Act* (Ch. 32).

[207] See section 23(4) of the *Coroners Act* (Ch. 32).

[208] See *R v Coroner for North Humberside and Scunthorpe; ex parte Jamieson* [1995] 1 QB 1, (1994) 158 JP 1011 and *The Queen on the Application of the Commissioner of Police for the Metropolis v Her Majesty's Coroner for Southern District of Greater London* [2003] EWHC Admin 1829.

[209] See *McKerr v Armagh Coroner and others* [1990] 1 All ER 865 and *Re an Application by McKerr for Judicial Review* (Unrep. UKHC, 2 June 1992).

COURT PROCEDURE

Where it appears to a Coroner that it is necessary or desirable, a coronial inquest concerning the death of a person may be commenced or held on a Sunday.[210]

If the Coroner considers it necessary he or she may adjourn a coronial inquest.

[2.0] OPEN COURT

A coronial inquest should ordinarily be held in public.[211]

Where in the opinion of the Coroner the interests of public morality require that any person should be excluded from the room or place where the Coroner is holding a coronial inquest, he or she may exclude such persons from the room or place[212], other than:

- a legal representative[213];

  or

- a representative of a newspaper[214].

At common law a Coroner may also exclude specific individuals or the public generally in the interests of justice, decency and order.[215]

---

210 See section 15 of the *Coroners Act* (Ch. 32).

211 See *R v Devine; ex parte Walton* [1930] 2 KB 29.

212 See section 30(1) of the *Coroners Act* (Ch. 32).

213 See section 30(2) of the *Coroners Act* (Ch. 32).

214 See section 30(3)(a) of the *Coroners Act* (Ch. 32).

215 See section 6 of the *Coroners Act* (Ch. 32).

See also: *Garnett v Ferrand* (1827) 6 B & C 611, (1829) 108 ER 576.

In respect of a coronial inquest involving a death the Coroner may also give such a ruling based on the consideration of what is due to the family of the deceased.[216]

Subject to the discretion of the Coroner, a person summonsed as a witness shall not be permitted to be present in the room or place where a Coroner is holding a coronial inquest, except:

- when the witness is giving evidence;

  or

- after the witness has given his or her evidence.[217]

[3.0] MEDIA

In relation to representatives of the media the Coroner may make an order forbidding the publication of any report or account of the evidence or other proceedings in a coronial inquest.[218]

---

[216] See section 6 of the *Coroners Act* (Ch. 32).

See also: *Garnett v Ferrand* (1827) 6 B & C 611, (1829) 108 ER 576.

[217] See section 29(1) of the *Coroners Act* (Ch. 32).

[218] See section 30(3)(b) of the *Coroners Act* (Ch. 32).

Failure to comply with such an order constitutes an offence, see section 30(4) of the *Coroners Act* (Ch. 32).

However, the National Court has the power to override such an order.

Such an order should only be made:

- if it is reasonably necessary to secure the proper administration of justice;

  and

- if there is some material upon which the Coroner can reasonably reach that conclusion.[219]

Whilst the media will always argue that the public has the right to know, the Coroner must balance:

- the public's right to know

  against

- the right of interested parties who may be affected by such reporting.

A Coroner should avoid contact with the media upon the commencement of a coronial inquest.

Furthermore, it is quite improper for a member of the media to telephone any person holding a judicial office.[220]

---

[219] See *John Fairfax and Sons v Police Tribunal* [1986] 5 NSWLR 465, per McHugh JA at 476-477.

See also: *Fairfax Publications Pty Ltd v Abernethy* [1999] NSWSC 826 and *Mirror Newspapers Limited v Waller* [1985] 1 NSWLR 1 at 25.

[220] See *Von Emein v Ahern* (Unrep. SAFC 2 February 1988).

COURT PROCEDURE

[4.0] RULES OF EVIDENCE

Considering that a coronial inquest is not a criminal trial or civil hearing, the Coroner can hear evidence that would otherwise be inadmissible in such a trial or hearing.

Quite unlike a criminal trial there is:

- no prosecution;
- no defence;
- no trial;

and the procedures and rules of evidence suitable for a trial are unsuitable for a coronial inquest.[221]

Whilst it is clear that a Coroner holding a coronial inquest is not bound by the strict rules of evidence[222], such rules should usually be observed[223].

A Coroner may admit any evidence that he or she thinks fit, even if it would be inadmissible in a criminal trial or civil hearing.

---

221 See *R v Her Majesty's Coroner for North Humberside and Scunthorpe; ex parte Jamieson* [1995] QB 1 at 17, (1994) 158 JP 1011 and *R v South London Coroner; ex parte Thompson* (1982) 126 SJ 625.

222 See *Devine v Attorney General for Northern Ireland* [1992] 1 All ER 609, per Lord Goff at 613; *R v Greater Manchester Coroner; ex parte Tal* [1985] 1 QB 67, per Robert Hoff LJ at 84; *R v Her Majesty's Coroner for Lincolnshire; ex parte Annette Hay (In Re: Brett Andrew Hay deceased)* [1999] EWHC Admin 155; *McKerr v Armagh Coroner and others* [1990] 1 All ER 865, per Lord Goff at 869 and *R v South London Coroner; ex parte Thompson* (1982) 126 SJ 625.

See also: Jervis on Coroners, 9th edition, 1957, page 508.

223 See Halsbury's Laws of England, 4th edition, Volume 9(2), page 534.

COURT PROCEDURE

Considering the ordinary rules of evidence do not apply to a coronial inquest the effect of this is twofold:

- it enlarges the scope of the inquiry;

  and

- it leads simply to the proper investigation of possibly suspicious circumstances.[224]

The evidence taken before a coronial inquest should always be:

- relevant;

  and

- logically probative[225],

thereby enabling the findings, comments and recommendations to be based upon material that tends logically to show:

- the existence or non-existence of facts relevant to the issue to be determined;

  or

- the likelihood of the occurrence of some future event the occurrence of which would be relevant[226].

---

[224] See Halsbury's Laws of England, 3rd edition, Volume 9(2), page 236.

[225] See *T A Miller Ltd v Minister of Housing and Local Government* [1968] 1 WLR 992 at 995.

[226] See *R v Deputy Industrial Injuries Commissioner; ex parte Moore* [1965] 1 QB 456 at 488.

See also: *Pochi v Minister for Immigration and Ethnic Affairs* (1979) 36 FLR 482 at 492.

It is then for the Coroner to give whatever 'weight'[227] or 'probative force' is appropriate to the evidence when handing down his or her findings, comments and recommendations.

A Coroner should also follow the 'best evidence rule'[228] and seek the production of original documents, where possible.

The Coroner may disallow evidence on the grounds of expediency[229], but he or she should not normally consider the evidence in private[230].

[5.0] RULES OF NATURAL JUSTICE

It is clear that a coronial inquest must be held in compliance with the rules of natural justice[231] or procedural fairness[232], and therefore avoid practical injustice[233].[234]

---

[227] Questions as to the weight of evidence are not determined by arbitrary rules, but by common sense, logic and experience, see *Dalu v R* [1993] SBHC 54.

[228] See *Kajala v Noble* (1982) 75 Cr App R 149, per Ackner LJ at 152.

[229] See *R v Her Majesty's Coroner for West Yorkshire (Eastern District); ex parte Clements* (1993) 138 JP 17.

[230] See *R v Her Majesty's Coroner for Inner North London District; ex parte Cohen* (1993) 158 JP 644.

See also: Halsbury's Laws of England, 4th edition, Volume 9(2), page 534.

[231] See *R v Doogan; ex parte Lucas-Smith and others* (2006) 158 ACTR 1 at 5, [2005] ACTSC 74.

[232] See *Maksimovich v Walsh* [1985] 4 NSWLR 318, per Kirby P at 327 and Samuels JA at 337.

[233] See *Minister for Immigration and Multicultural Affairs; Re ex parte Lam* [2003] HCA 6.

[234] See also: *Harmsworth v The State Coroner* [1989] VR 989 and *R v Electricity Commissioners; ex parte London Electricity Joint Committee Co (1920) Ltd* [1924] 1 KB 171.

COURT PROCEDURE

The principles of natural justice are the rules of the underlying law known by that name developed for control of judicial and administrative proceedings.[235]

Fairness is essentially a practical concept. It is not abstract in nature. The law of procedural fairness is concerned to avoid practical injustice.[236]

However, the requirements of natural justice are flexible and vary with the circumstances of each case.[237]

Furthermore, simply because an interested party is not present at a coronial inquest the presiding Coroner is not excused from his or her duty to accord that interested party natural justice.[238]

One of the rules of the underlying law relating to the control of judicial and administrative proceedings is the principle of natural justice the maximum requirement of which is:

> to not only act fairly, but to be seen to act fairly[239].[240]

---

[235] See section 59(1) of the *Constitution of the Independent State of Papua New Guinea*.

[236] See *Re Minister for Immigration and Multicultural and Indigenous Affairs; ex parte Lam* (2003) 214 CLR 1, [2003] HCA 6, per Gleeson CJ.

[237] See *Kioa v West* (1985) 159 CLR 550 at 584; *Musumeci v Attorney-General of New South Wales and another* (2003) 57 NSWLR 193; [2003] NSWCA 77, per Ipp JA with whom Beazley JA agreed; *Russell v Norfolk (Duke)* [1949] 1 All ER 109 at 118; *Mobil Oil Australia Pty Ltd v Federal Commissioner of Taxation* (1963) 113 CLR 475 at 504, [1963] HCA 41 and *McNab v Auburn Soccer Sports Club Ltd* [1975] 1 NSWLR 54 at 59-60.

[238] See *Director of National Parks and Wildlife v Dennis Joseph Barritt SM, a Coroner for the Northern Territory of Australia and Attorney-General for the Northern Territory of Australia* (1990) 72 NTR 1, [1990] NTSC 37.

[239] See section 59(2) of the *Constitution of the Independent State of Papua New Guinea*.

[240] See *Sela Gipe v The State* [2000] PNGLR 271, [2000] PGSC 28.

COURT PROCEDURE

Procedural fairness includes a requirement that the decision-making process of a Coroner be free from:

- actual;

  or

- apprehended bias.[241]

An allegation of bias is serious because it affects the requirement for impartiality by a Court in the administration of justice.[242]

A Court should ascertain all of the legal and factual merits for such an application.[243]

The apprehension must be 'firmly established'.[244]

---

[241] See *Honda Australia Motorcycle and others v Johnstone (as State Coroner) and others* [2005] VSC 387.

As regards extra-curial contact, see *R v Ian Roger Matterson; ex parte Christine Debra Moles* [1994] Tas R 87.

[242] See *Boateng v The State* [1990] PNGLR 342; *PNG Pipes Pty Ltd and Sankaran Venugopal v Mujo Sefa, Globes Pty Ltd and Romy Macasaet* (1998) SC592, [1998] PGSC 52 and *Coecon Limited (Receiver/Manager Appointed) v The National Fisheries Authority of Papua New Guinea and Independent State of Papua New Guinea* (2002) N2182.

In the context of a criminal proceedings, refer also to the section titled 'Right To An Independent And Impartial Court' in the chapter titled 'Rights Of A Defendant' in the text titled 'Injia on Criminal Practice and Procedure in Papua New Guinea and the Pacific'.

[243] See *Ebner v Official Trustee in Bankruptcy* (2000) 205 CLR 337 at 363, [2000] HCA 63 and *Re Medicaments and Related Classes of Goods (No. 2)* [2001] 1 WLR 700.

[244] See *Re J.R.L.; ex parte C.J.L.* (1986) 161 CLR 342, per Mason J at 352, [1986] HCA 39; *Re Watson; ex parte Armstrong* (1976) 136 CLR 248 at 262, [1976] HCA 39; *Re Shaw; ex parte Shaw* (1980) 55 ALJR 12 at 14 and *R v Commonwealth Conciliation and Arbitration Commission; ex parte Angliss Group* (1969) 122 CLR 546 at 553, [1969] HCA 10.

Such an application must not be based on assertions.[245]

There must be a proper basis for such an application based on reasonable, not fanciful, unprincipled, frivolous or futile, grounds.[246]

There may be a 'reasonable apprehension' of bias if a Coroner is considered to have acted 'improperly, unfairly or unreasonably'.[247]

An application made without any proper factual and legal foundation amounts to scandalising the Court which is contemptuous.[248]

[6.0] CORONER'S ASSISTANT

The person assisting the Coroner plays a supportive and investigatory role.

---

[245] See *PNG Pipes Pty Ltd and Sankaran Venugopal v Mujo Sefa, Globes Pty Ltd and Romy Macasaet* (1998) SC592, [1998] PGSC 52; *Gobe Hongu Ltd v National Executive Council and others* (1999) N1920 and *The State v Puli A'aron* (2003) N2432, [2003] PGNC 75.

See also: *Raybos Australia Pty Ltd v Tectran Corp Pty Ltd (No. 4)* [1986] 6 NSWLR 674 at 689.

[246] See *Denden Tom and others v The State* (2008) SC967; *PNG Pipes Pty Ltd and Sankaran Venugapal v Mujo Sefa, Globes Pty Ltd and Romy Macasaet* (1998) SC592, [1998] PGSC 52; *Review pursuant to Constitution, Section 155(2)(b); Application by Herman Joseph Leahy* (2006) SC981, [2006] PGSC 37; *Thomas Kavali v Thomas Hoihoi* [1984] PNGLR 182; *Boateng v The State* [1990] PNGLR 342; *Sela Gipe v The State* [2000] PNGLR 271, [2000] PGSC 28; *Danny Yai v Joseph Pindu* (2009) N3630; *The State v Peter Sari* [1990] PNGLR 48 and *The State v Stuart Fancy* (1994) N1264.

[247] See *Evans v Milton* (1979) 24 OR (2d) 181, 97 DLR (3d) 687; *People First of Ontario v Porter, Regional Coroner Niagara* (1991) 5 OR (3d) 609, (1991) 85 DLR (4th) 174; sub nom *People First of Ontario v Niagara (Regional Coroner)* at 617 and 182 [reversed on other grounds (1992) 6 OR (3d) 289, (1992) 87 DLR (4th) 765].

See also: See *R v Doogan; ex parte Lucas-Smith and others* (2006) 158 ACTR 1 at 5, [2005] ACTSC 74.

[248] See *Denden Tom and others v The State* (2008) SC967.

COURT PROCEDURE

Depending on the nature of a coronial inquest the Coroner's Assistant should either be:

- a qualified police prosecutor[249];

  or

- a lawyer from the Attorney-General's department.

It is the responsibility of a Coroner's Assistant to assist the Coroner in holding a coronial inquest by:

- arranging the attendance of witnesses, as required by the Coroner;
- calling the witnesses as selected by the Coroner to give evidence in the order as determined by the Coroner;
- conducting examination of witnesses, as deemed necessary;
- tendering the statements of witnesses who are not to be called as exhibits;
- tendering any other exhibits to the Court;

  and

- making a submission in order to assist the Coroner to make appropriate findings, comments and recommendations at the discretion of the Coroner.

[249] See *R v Ian Roger Matterson; ex parte Christine Debra Moles* [1994] 4 Tas R 87.

COURT PROCEDURE

[7.0] INTERESTED PARTY

When the Coroner considers:

- that a person, whether subpoenaed as a witness or not, has a particular interest in a coronial inquest;

  or

- the conduct or act of such a person is in any way material to the subject-matter of a coronial inquest,

he or she may permit the witness to be present in the room or place where the coronial inquest is being held.[250]

Such a person is entitled:

- to be represented by a legal representative;

  and

- to examine or cross-examine witnesses in relation to the subject-matter of the coronial inquest.[251]

An interested party must however first seek standing[252] with the leave of the Coroner in order to appear and be legally represented.

---

[250] See section 29(2) of the *Coroners Act* (Ch. 32).

[251] See section 29(3) of the *Coroners Act* (Ch. 32).

[252] See *Wolfe v Robinson* [1961] OR 250, (1961) 27 DLR (2d) 98, (1961) 129 CCC 361, aff'd [1962] OR 132, (1962) 31 DLR (2d) 233, (1962) 132 CCC 78.

The test to be adopted on the issue of 'locus standi' is that in order to entertain such an application the applicant ought to have a 'sufficient interest' in the proceedings.[253]

Leave may be given to a legally recognised entity such as a government department or registered company.

However, a person or legal entity that merely has a financial interest in the outcome of a coronial inquest may not necessarily have the right to appear. It will be at the discretion of the Coroner as to whether there is sufficient interest or standing.

Public interest advocacy groups may seek standing although such groups have no knowledge or connection with the individuals involved, but may be able to play a special role depending on the nature of the coronial inquest.[254]

A person who may have a particular interest in a coronial inquest, includes:

- the Attorney-General;
- a person who is implicated in the commission of an alleged offence[255] that is related to:
    - the 'manner' and 'cause' of the death of a person;
    - the 'cause' and 'origin' of a fire;

    or

[253] See *NTN Pty Ltd v Board of Post and Telecommunication Corporation and others* [1987] PNGLR 70; *Arowe Logging Pty Ltd v The Independent State of Papua New Guinea and Minister for Forest* [1988-89] PNGLR 216 and *PNG Air Pilots v Director of Civil Aviation* [1983] PGNLR 1.

[254] See *People First of Ontario v Porter, Regional Coroner Niagara* (1991) 5 OR (3d) 609, (1991) 85 DLR (4th) 174; sub nom *People First of Ontario v Niagara (Regional Coroner)* at 617 and 182 [reversed on other grounds (1992) 6 OR (3d) 289, (1992) 87 DLR (4th) 765].

[255] See section 19 of the *Coroners Act* (Ch. 32).

- the disappearance of a missing person;

and

- a person against whom civil action could be taken.

A legal representative who is denied right of appearance may:

- be permitted to sit at the bar table in order to watch the interests of their client;

and

- be permitted to ask questions to specific witnesses, but not generally.

In compliance with the rules of natural justice:

- a person who has been adversely implicated in the commission of an alleged offence should be:
    - given notice of the proceedings[256];
    - given the opportunity to be legally represented[257];
    - given a copy of the relevant material, unless the withholding of the material is necessary in order to protect the integrity of the coronial inquest[258];

---

[256] See *International Finance Trust Co Ltd v New South Wales Crime Commission* (2009) 240 CLR 319, [2009] HCA 49.

[257] See section 29(3) of the *Coroners Act* (Ch. 32).

[258] See *Musumeci v Attorney General of New South Wales and another* (2003) 57 NSWLR 193, [2003] NSWCA 77 and *International Finance Trust Co Ltd v New South Wales Crime Commission* (2009) 240 CLR 319, [2009] HCA 49.

- given an opportunity to give evidence[259];

- given the opportunity to have witnesses called[260];

- given the opportunity to cross-examine witnesses[261], provided that such questions are for the purpose of assisting in establishing the matters that the coronial inquest is to determine[262];

  and

- given the right to be heard[263] and be able to make a submission prior to being committed to appear in the National Court[264];

and

[259] See section 19 of the *Coroners Act* (Ch. 32).

See also: *The King v Scorey* (1748) 1 Leach 43 and *Wakley v Cooke* (1849) 4 Exch. 511, 154 ER 1316.

[260] See section 29(3) of the *Coroners Act* (Ch. 32).

See also: *Sakawar Kasieng v Andrew Baigry, Magistrate of Wewak District Court and the State* (2004) N2562 and *International Finance Trust Co Ltd v New South Wales Crime Commission* (2009) 240 CLR 319, [2009] HCA 49.

[261] See section 29(3) of the *Coroners Act* (Ch. 32).

See also: *International Finance Trust Co Ltd v New South Wales Crime Commission* (2009) 240 CLR 319, [2009] HCA 49.

[262] See *R v Hammersmith Coroner; ex parte Peach* [1980] 1 QB 211, per Griffiths J at 220.

[263] See *International Finance Trust Co Ltd v New South Wales Crime Commission* (2009) 240 CLR 319, [2009] HCA 49.

[264] See *Sakawar Kasieng v Andrew Baigry, Magistrate of Wewak District Court and the State* (2004) N2562.

- a person against whom civil action could be taken should be:
  - contacted;
  - given the opportunity to be legally represented[265];

    and
  - given the opportunity to cross-examine witnesses[266], provided that such questions are for the purpose of assisting in establishing the matters that the coronial inquest is to determine[267].

Whilst a Coroners Assistant or a legal representative representing an interested party[268], have no right to make a submission to the Coroner at the conclusion of a coronial inquest, the rules of natural justice should be applied.

A Coroner may find it useful to receive such submissions on aspects of the law and/or facts, if the Coroner requires a direction on a point of law or clarification of a version of facts.

This is however purely at the discretion of the Coroner.

An interested party does not have the automatic right to address the Court on matters unconnected with any contemplated unfavourable finding which is adverse to that party's interests.[269]

---

265 See section 29(3) of the *Coroners Act* (Ch. 32).

266 See section 29(3) of the *Coroners Act* (Ch. 32).

267 See *R v Hammersmith Coroner; ex parte Peach* [1980] 1 QB 211, per Griffiths J at 220.

268 See *The State v Jacob Toroken, Coroner; ex parte George Nelson Perera* (1981) N281.

269 See *Annetts v McCann* (1990) 170 CLR 596, per Brennan J at 610, [1990] HCA 57.

The relevant rule of natural justice only affords such a person who may be potentially adversely affected by a particular finding to address on that issue.[270]

[8.0] OATH, SOLEMN DECLARATION AND AFFIRMATION

All witnesses must be examined under oath or after making a solemn declaration or affirmation.[271]

The oath is as follows:

> 'The evidence that you give to the court touching the matters in question between the parties will be the truth, the whole truth and nothing but the truth. So help you God!'[272]

A witness who:

- objects to taking an oath;
- is reasonably objected to as incompetent to take an oath;
- appears to the court incompetent to take an oath;

  or

[270] See *R v Tennent; ex parte Jager* (2000) 9 Tas R 111, [2000] TASSC 64.

[271] See sections 10(a), 17(3) and 20(3) of the *Coroners Act* (Ch. 32).

[272] See section 2 of the *Oaths, Affirmations and Statutory Declaration Act* (Ch. 317).

- desires or is required to take an oath in a form and manner required by his or her religion to make it binding on his or her conscience, but which it is found to be impracticable to administer to him or her in that form and manner at the time when, and the place where, the oath is desire or required to be taken

may, instead of taking an oath, make a solemn declaration or affirmation in Form 9.

The wording of the solemn declaration or affirmation is as follows:

> 'I solemnly (declare or affirm[273]) that the evidence now about to be given [...] by me is the truth, whole truth and nothing but the truth'.

[9.0] COMPETENCY AND COMPELLABILITY

[9.1] DEATH AND FIRE CORONIAL INQUEST

The provisions of the *Evidence Act* (Ch. 48) regarding the right of a defendant, and the husband or wife of a defendant to give evidence or otherwise, extend to proceedings before a Coroner and apply as such to a coronial inquest, but do not apply to an inquiry into the cause and circumstances of the disappearance of a missing person.[274]

---

[273] However, that form is inconsistent with section 5(2) of the *Oaths, Affirmations and Statutory Declaration Act* (Ch. 317) which provides for the making of a solemn declaration or affirmation.

Section 27(1) of the *Interpretation Act* (Ch. 2) provides that substantial compliance with a form contained in a provision is sufficient.

In order for the form to be consistent with section 5(2) the words 'or affirm' have been included.

[274] See section 24 of the *Coroners Act* (Ch. 32).

COURT PROCEDURE

A person charged with an offence is a competent, but not a compellable, witness for himself or herself in any legal proceedings in connexion with the offence with which he or she is charged.[275]

The wife or husband[276] of a person charged with an offence is a competent witness in any legal proceedings in connexion with the offence.[277]

However, the wife or husband of a person charged with an offence shall not be called as a witness in any legal proceedings in connexion with the offence without consent of his or her spouse, except:

- where the wife or husband, as the case may be, is compellable to give evidence[278];

  or

---

[275] See section 19(1)(a) of the *Coroners Act* (Ch. 32) and section 12 of the *Evidence Act* (Ch. 48).

[276] The terms 'husband' and 'wife' in section 13 of the *Evidence Act* (Ch. 48) mean:

- a person to whom the defendant is married in accordance with Part V of the *Marriage Act* (Ch. 280);
  or
- a person with whom the defendant has entered into a customary marriage, see *The State v James Yali* (2005) N2931, [2005] PGNC 24.

[277] See section 13(1) of the *Evidence Act* (Ch. 48).

[278] The common law rule is that a spouse is an incompetent witness in criminal proceedings in which the other spouse is a defendant, except where the defendant spouse is charged with a serious offence involving violence to a child under the age of 16 years who is residing under their care in their matrimonial home, see *SCR No. 3 of 1985; The State v Uniss Kamugaip* [1985] PNGLR 278 at 280, [1985] PGSC 5.

- where the husband or wife is charged with being a party to an offence against the other[279].[280]

[9.2] MISSING PERSON CORONIAL INQUEST

A person who:

- has, alleges or has alleged that he or she has, knowledge or information concerning a matter or thing relevant to an inquiry into the cause and circumstances of the disappearance of a missing person;

  or

- the Coroner has reason to be believe has, is alleging or has alleged that he or she has such knowledge or information

is a competent and compellable witness as to the knowledge or information and the sources from which he or she obtained it.[281]

---

[279] See *Wemp Mapa and three others v The State* [1979] PNGLR 135, [1979] PGSC 15; *SCR No. 3 of 1985; The State v Uniss Kamugaip* [1985] PNGLR 278 at 280, [1985] PGSC 5 and *The State v Tu'uo Ibru* (1999) N1940.

The common law rule is that a spouse is an incompetent witness in criminal proceedings in which the other spouse is a defendant, except where the charge involves the person, liberty or health of the witness spouse, see *Lord Audley's Case* [1631] Hutt 115, 123 ER 1140 at 1141; *Bentley v Cooke* (1784) 3 Doug KB 422, 99 ER 729 and *R v Bissell* [1882] 1 OR 514.

[280] See section 13(2) of the *Evidence Act* (Ch. 48).

[281] See section 20(2) of the *Coroners Act* (Ch. 32).

[10.0] PRIVILEGE AGAINST SELF-INCRIMINATION

The *Coroners Act* (Ch. 32) does not make a person compellable to answer a question tending to incriminate himself or herself.[282]

However, a witness cannot refuse to go into the witness box on the ground that he or she might incriminate himself or herself.[283]

A witness can only claim the privilege:

- after being sworn in;

  and

- in relation to specific questions.[284]

The privilege strictly applies only to answering and does not prevent the relevant question being asked.[285]

A witness must honestly believe that by answering the question he or she will or may incriminate himself or herself.[286]

---

282 See section 27(a) of the *Coroners Act* (Ch. 32).

283 See *R v Her Majesty's Coroner for Lincolnshire; ex parte Annette Hay (In Re: Brett Andrew Hay deceased)* [1999] EWHC Admin 155, (1999) 163 JP 666.

284 See *R v Her Majesty's Coroner for Lincolnshire; ex parte Annette Hay (In Re: Brett Andrew Hay deceased)* [1999] EWHC Admin 155, (1999) 163 JP 666 and *R v Her Majesty's Coroner for Derby and South Derbyshire; ex parte Hart* (2000) 164 JP 429.

285 See *R v Her Majesty's Coroner for Lincolnshire; ex parte Annette Hay (In Re: Brett Andrew Hay deceased)* [1999] EWHC Admin 155, (1999) 163 JP 666.

286 See *R v Her Majesty's Coroner for Lincolnshire; ex parte Annette Hay (In Re: Brett Andrew Hay deceased)* [1999] EWHC Admin 155, (1999) 163 JP 666.

It is however for the Coroner to decide whether the witness is entitled to the privilege.[287]

In order to invoke the privilege the Coroner must be satisfied that the answer would tend to incriminate the witness.[288]

Except in proceedings for an offence against the *Coroners Act* (Ch. 32), a statement or disclosure made by a witness on an inquiry into the cause and circumstances of the disappearance of a missing person in answer to a question put to him or her or before the Coroner is not admissible in evidence against the witness in any civil or criminal proceedings.[289]

[11.0] PROTECTION OF WITNESSES

In exceptional cases if the administration of justice so requires a Coroner may make orders permitting:

- the admission of an anonymous written statement, if the safety of the witness is in jeopardy[290];
- the screening of a witness[291];

[287] See *R v Her Majesty's Coroner for Lincolnshire; ex parte Annette Hay (In Re: Brett Andrew Hay deceased)* [1999] EWHC Admin 155, (1999) 163 JP 666.

[288] See *R v Her Majesty's Coroner for Lincolnshire; ex parte Annette Hay (In Re: Brett Andrew Hay deceased)* [1999] EWHC Admin 155, (1999) 163 JP 666.

[289] See section 20(5) of the *Coroners Act* (Ch. 32).

[290] See *R v Her Majesty's Attorney-General for Northern Ireland; ex parte Devine* [1992] 1 WLR 262.

[291] See *R v Her Majesty's Coroner for Newcastle upon Tyne; Ex parte "A" (A police officer of Northumbria Police Force)* [1997] EWHC Admin 1172 and *R v Watford Magistrates' Court; ex parte Lenman* [1993] Crim LR 388.

and/or

- the use of a pseudonym by a witness[292].

[12.0] EXAMINATION OF WITNESSES

The Coroner has complete control of a coronial inquest and may therefore, ask any question of a witness at any time.

Unlike a trial, where a Court normally does not, on its own volition call a witness, a coronial inquest is similar to a commission of inquiry which is at total freedom to inquire into all the possible factors that are considered relevant to the Coroner.[293]

A Coroner holding a coronial inquest concerning the death of a person shall examine on oath[294] or solemn declaration or affirmation all persons:

- whom he or she thinks fit to examine;
- who tender their evidence;

  or

- who, in his or her opinion, are able to give relevant evidence

292 See *Morris v Dublin City Coroner* [2000] IESC 24, [2000] 3 IR 603, [2001] 1 ILRM 125 and *The person identified at the inquest into death of Joseph Gilewicz as Sierra 4 v Christine Debra Moles, Commissioner of Police and the Attorney-General (Tas); Commissioner of Police v Christine Debra Moles and the person identified at the inquest into the death of Joseph Gilewicz as Sierra 4 and Attorney-General (Tas)* [1994] TASSC 38.

293 See *Sakawar Kasieng v Andrew Baigry, Magistrate of Wewak District Court and the State* (2004) N2562.

294 Section 3(1) of the *Interpretation Act* (Ch. 2) defines the term 'oath' in the *Coroners Act* (Ch. 32) as including the making of a solemn declaration or affirmation.

respecting the facts concerning the death.[295]

A Coroner holding a coronial inquest into the cause and origin of a fire shall examine on oath[296] or solemn declaration or affirmation all persons:

- whom he or she thinks fit to examine;
- who tender their evidence;

  or

- who, in his or her opinion, may be able to give any relevant evidence

respecting the facts concerning the fire.[297]

A Coroner holding an inquiry into the cause and circumstances of the disappearance of a missing person shall examine on oath[298] or solemn declaration or affirmation all persons:

- whom he or she thinks fit to examine;
- who tender their evidence;

  or

- who, in his or her opinion, are able to give relevant evidence

---

[295] See section 10(a) of the *Coroners Act* (Ch. 32).

[296] The term 'oath' in the *Coroners Act* (Ch. 32) includes the making of a solemn declaration or affirmation, see section 3(1) of the *Interpretation Act* (Ch. 2).

[297] See section 17(3) of the *Coroners Act* (Ch. 32).

[298] The term 'oath' in the *Coroners Act* (Ch. 32) includes the making of a solemn declaration or affirmation, see section 3(1) of the *Interpretation Act* (Ch. 2).

respecting the facts concerning the disappearance of a missing person.[299]

At a coronial inquest a witness is not called by an interested party.[300]

If there are several persons entitled to examine witnesses, it is at the discretion of the Coroner, after consultation with the interested parties, as to the order of cross-examination.[301]

It is usual practice upon the calling of a witness for the Coroner or Coroner's Assistant to ask the witness the following questions upon the witness being shown his or her written statement by the Coroner's Assistant:

- Is that your statement?;
- Is that your signature at the bottom of the statement?;
- Is the statement written in a language that you can read and understand?;
- Did you read the statement?;

  or

- Was the statement read to you?; and By whom?
- Did you understand the contents of the statement before you signed it?;
- Is your statement true and correct?;

[299] See section 20(3) of the *Coroners Act* (Ch. 32).

[300] See *R v South London Coroner; ex parte Thompson* (1982) 126 SJ 625, per Lane LCJ and *McKerr v Armagh Coroner and others* [1990] 1 All ER 865, per Lord Goff at 869.

[301] See Halsbury's Laws of England, 4th edition, Volume 9(2), page 537.

and

- Do you wish to make any alteration to your statement?

If a witness is unable to confirm whether he or she made a written statement upon being shown the statement by the Coroner's Assistant, the Coroner or Coroner's Assistant is required to:

- read the statement to the witness;

  and

- ask the abovementioned questions.

Such responses are recorded and the written statement is then put into evidence as an exhibit if confirmed as the statement of the witness.

The witness may then be examined upon his or her statement, at the discretion of the Coroner[302], but subject to the rules of natural justice.

For obvious reasons, a leading question[303] should not be asked in relation to matters that are likely to be in dispute, and particularly in matters relating to possible criminal offences.

Unless the Coroner otherwise determines, a witness at a coronial inquest should be examined first by the Coroner or Coroner's Assistant and, if the witness is legally represented, lastly by his or her legal representative.[304]

---

[302] See *The State v Jacob Toroken, Coroner; ex parte George Nelson Perera* (1981) N281.

[303] A 'leading question' is simply a question that puts something in the mouth of a witness before the witness actually says it, see *Saunders* (1985) 15 A Crim R 115.

[304] See Halsbury's Laws of England, 4th edition, Volume 9(2), page 537.

COURT PROCEDURE

A legal representative should not be given the opportunity to use a coronial inquest as an opportunity to obtain evidence for:

- future civil proceedings[305];

  or

- future criminal proceedings.[306]

Upon closure of the questioning by the legal representatives representing any interested parties it is usual practice for the Coroner or Coroner's Assistant to ask the final questions in order to clarify any facts or issues.

When there is a person who appears responsible for a death or fire it is usual practice to call that person last. This person will usually refuse to answer questions on the grounds of self-incrimination.

Whilst it is not necessary for all witnesses to an incident to be called to give evidence in a coronial inquest[307], it would be irregular for a Coroner to accept as the evidence of a witness, a previously prepared written statement, without examining the witness under oath or solemn affirmation or declaration.

A written statement of a witness not called to be examined may however be tendered as an exhibit and used as evidence in a coronial inquest.

---

[305] See *Huynh and Huynh v Dr. Jones et al.* (1991) 2 OR (3d) 562, per McRuer CJ at 565.

[306] See *Poplar Coroner; ex parte Thomas* [1993] QB 610, [1993] 2 All ER 381, per Dillon LJ at 629 and 387.

[307] See Coronial Law and Practice in New South Wales, 3rd edition, page 101.

[13.0] STATEMENTS AND REPORTS

A written statement may:

- be used as the basis upon which a witness can be examined;

  and

- form part of the depositions of a coronial inquest.[308]

It is entirely at the discretion of the Coroner as to what use statements are to be used at a coronial inquest.[309]

A copy of all documentary material relevant to a coronial inquest should be made available to all persons granted attendance at such a proceedings[310], subject to public interest immunity not applying thereto.[311]

Public interest immunity is concerned only with the conduct of governmental functions.[312]

---

308 See *Re Ford's Inquest* [1956] NZ LR 805.

309 See *Peach v Commissioner of Police* [1986] 2 All ER 129, per Fox LJ at 138.

310 See *Maksimovich v Walsh* [1985] 4 NSWLR 318, per Kirby J at 328.

311 See *Musumeci v Attorney-General of New South Wales and another* (2003) 57 NSWLR 193, [2003] NSWCA 77, per Young CJ and *Taylor v Anderton* [1995] 1 WLR 447.

See however: *R v Hammersmith Coroner; ex parte Peach* [1980] 1 QB 211, per Widgery LCJ at 218.

312 See *R v Young* [1999] NSWCCA 166.

Refer also to the chapter titled 'Public Interest Immunity' in the text titled 'Injia on Criminal Practice and Procedure in Papua New Guinea and the Pacific'.

Public interest immunity arises because of the need to safeguard the proper functioning of the executive arm of government and of the public service.[313]

Access should also be given to documentation upon which an expert bases his or her report.[314]

A Coroner is not obliged to require the police to disclose any statements or reports in their possession in advance of a coronial inquest[315], but may do so.

---

[313] See *Sankey v Whitlam* (1978) 142 CLR 1 at 56, [1978] HCA 43; *Commonwealth v Northern Land Council* (1993) 176 CLR 604 at 619, [1993] HCA 24 and *R v Young* [1999] NSWCCA 166.

[314] See *R v Doogan; ex parte Lucas-Smith and others* [2004] ACTSC 91.

[315] See *R v Hammersmith Coroner; ex parte Peach* [1980] QB 211 and *R v Her Majesty's Coroner for Lincolnshire; ex parte Annette Hay (In Re: Brett Andrew Hay deceased)* [1999] EWHC Admin 155.

FINDINGS

[1.0] INTRODUCTION[316]

A Coroner before whom a coronial inquest is held shall:

- make an abstract of the proceedings on the coronial inquest and his or her findings[317];
- state in the abstract the names of all witnesses examined at the coronial inquest;

  and

- annex to the abstract:
  - an account of all sums of money ordered or certified by him or her to be paid on account of the coronial inquest;

    and

  - an account of the number of days during which the coronial inquest or any adjournment of the coronial inquest continued.[318]

The Coroner shall certify the abstract and accounts to be true and correct and sign and transmit them without delay to the Attorney-General to be filed on record in such manner as the Minister directs.[319]

---

[316] See Coronial Law and Practice in New South Wales, 3rd edition.

[317] See section 1(h) and Form 8 of the *Coroners Regulation* (Ch. 32).

[318] See section 34(1) of the *Coroners Act* (Ch. 32).

[319] See section 34(2) of the *Coroners Act* (Ch. 32).

FINDINGS

After hearing the evidence in an inquiry into the cause and circumstances of the disappearance of a missing person the Coroner shall:

- give his or her decision or finding in writing signed by him or her[320];

  and

- forward the decision or finding to the Attorney-General together with the depositions.[321]

A finding delivered by a Coroner must be:

- based on the evidence given at the coronial inquest[322];

  and

- made with due regard to certain essential requirements of justice[323],

otherwise it constitutes a denial of natural justice, as well as an error of law.[324]

---

[320] See section 1(h) and Form 8 of the *Coroners Regulation* (Ch. 32).

[321] See section 20(4) of the *Coroners Act* (Ch. 32).

[322] See *Musumeci v Attorney-General of New South Wales and another* (2003) 57 NSWLR 193, [2003] NSWCA 77, per Young CJ; *Khan v Keown* [2001] VSCA 137; *York v General Medical Assessment Tribunal* [2003] 2 Qd R 104, [2002] QCA 519; *Herron v Attorney-General for New South Wales* (1987) 8 NSWLR 601, per McHugh JA at 617; *Bhattacharya v Hamilton* [2000] NSWSC 102 and *Veitch v The State Coroner* [2008] WASC 187.

[323] See *Attorney-General (NSW) v Mirror Newspapers Ltd* [1980] 1 NSWLR 374 at 385.

[324] See *Sinclair v Maryborough Mining Warden and another* (1974-1975) 132 CLR 473.

FINDINGS

Although a Coroner does not decide rights, evidence given to a Coroner may be used to support subsequent civil[325] or criminal proceedings[326], perhaps adversely to a witness. A Coroner's report certainly may have a real effect on reputation. A Coroner should not draw an adverse inference from failure to respond to evidence apparently critical of a witness.[327]

The decision must be based on material that tends logically to show:

- the existence;

  or

- the non-existence

of facts relevant to the issue to be determined.[328]

A Coroner should be as precise as possible in relation to his or her findings. Sometimes, however, an exact date or time cannot be established.

The use of the phrase 'on or about' covers the 'within a day or two' situations; whereas the use of the phrase 'between ... and ...' will cover longer periods of uncertainty.

---

[325] See *Huynh and Huynh v Dr. Jones et al.* (1991) 2 OR (3d) 562, per McRuer CJ at 565.

[326] See *Poplar Coroner; ex parte Thomas* [1993] QB 610, [1993] 2 All ER 381, per Dillon LJ at 629 and 387.

[327] See *S v The Director of Public Prosecutions and others* [2007] ACTSC 100.

[328] See *R v Deputy Industrial Injuries Commissioner; ex parte Moore* [1965] 1 QB 456 at 488.

FINDINGS

It is for the Coroner to determine:

- the relevance;

  and

- the weight

of the evidence given at an inquest.[329]

Whilst there is a duty imposed on the Courts to give reasons for their decisions, the reasons need not be extensive and in some cases little more may be required then a statement of the main conclusions on which the decision is based.[330]

There is nothing objectionable in a Coroner expressing a preliminary view, prior to making any findings and/or comments or recommendations.[331]

---

329 See *Minister for Immigration and Ethnic Affairs v Wu Shan Liang* (1996) 185 CLR 259 at 291, [1996] HCA 6.

See also: *Milu v WJ Smith, Coroner and Chief Executive, Queensland Transport and Attorney-General* [2003] QSC 430.

330 See *R v Doogan; ex parte Lucas-Smith and others* (2006) 158 ACTR 1, [2005] ACTSC 74; sub nom *Re Doogan; ex parte Lucas-Smith and others* (2005) 193 FLR 239, [2005] ACTSC 74.

331 See *Carruthers v Connolly* [1998] 1 Qd R 339, per Thomas J at 372 and *Laws v Australian Broadcasting Tribunal* (1990) 170 CLR 70 at 100, [1990] HCA 31.

See also: *Milu v WJ Smith, Coroner and Chief Executive, Queensland Transport and Attorney-General* [2003] QSC 430.

FINDINGS

In compliance with a rule of natural justice if a Coroner intends to make an adverse finding against any person the Court should ensure that the said person is so informed.[332]

[2.0] STANDARD OF PROOF

The standard of proof to be applied by the Coroner holding a coronial inquest is the civil standard of on the 'balance of probabilities'[333], other than for a finding of suicide which is one of 'beyond reasonable doubt'[334].

The degree of satisfaction can vary according to the gravity of the issue to be determined. A finding could have an extremely deleterious effect upon the character of a person, their reputation and employment prospects and accordingly, the weight of evidence demanded must be commensurate with gravity of the allegation[335].[336]

---

[332] See *Attorney-General v Maksimovich* [1985] 4 NSWLR 300, per Kirby P at 311-312 and *Director of National Parks and Wildlife v Dennis Joseph Barritt SM, a Coroner for the Northern Territory of Australia and Attorney-General for the Northern Territory of Australia* (1990) 72 NTR 1, [1990] NTSC 37.

[333] However, a Coroner's Court does not have to treat hypotheses that are reasonably available on the evidence as precluding it from reaching the conclusion that a particular fact is more probable than not, see *Briginshaw v Briginshaw* (1938) 60 CLR 336, [1938] HCA 34.

See also: *Plover v McIndoe* (2000) 2 VR 385, [2000] VSC 475; *Domaszewicz v The State Coroner* (2004) 11 VR 237, [2004] VSC 528; *Hurley v Clements* [2009] QCA 167 and *R v Her Majesty's Coroner for Inner South London District; ex parte Epsom Health Care NHS Trust* (1994) 158 JP 973.

[334] See *R v North Northumberland Coroner; ex parte Armstrong* (1987) 151 JP 773 at 785.

See also: *R v West London Coroner; ex parte Gray* [1988] QB 467; *R v Wolverhampton Coroner; ex parte McCurbin* [1990] 1 WLR 719 and Halsbury's Laws of England, 4th edition, Volume 9(2), page 543.

However, the civil standard applies in Australia.

[335] See *Anderson v Blashki* [1993] 2 VR 89.

[336] See The Function of the Coroner and the Coronial Jurisdiction, www.courts.act.gov.au.

FINDINGS

Where there is evidence of a criminal act proof of that act must be:

- clear;

  and

- cogent (convincing)

and when considering such proof weight must be given to the presumption of innocence.[337]

This imposes on the Court the burden of:

- reviewing the whole of the evidence;

  and

- examining for itself all issues of fact, including inferences from the evidence.[338]

In order to commit a person under the provisions of section 19 of the *Coroners Act* (Ch. 32) the Coroner should be satisfied that the evidence establishes a prima facie case.[339]

---

[337] See *Anderson v Blashki* [1993] 2 VR 89 and *Briginshaw v Briginshaw* (1938) 60 CLR 336, [1938] HCA 34.

[338] See *Anderson v Blashki* [1993] 2 VR 89 and *Briginshaw v Briginshaw* (1938) 60 CLR 336, [1938] HCA 34.

[339] See *The State v Michael Nama and others* (1999) N1884.

FINDINGS

[3.0] DEATH INQUEST

[3.1] INTRODUCTION

A Coroner holding a coronial inquest into the 'manner' and 'medical cause' of the death of a person shall after hearing the evidence, give his or her decision or findings and certify it in writing in the prescribed form[340], so far as such details have been proved, the following particulars:

- the identity of the deceased;

- how, when and where the deceased came by his or her death;

  and

- the person (if any) suspected or accused of having caused the death by the commission of the offences of Wilful Murder[341], Murder[342] or Manslaughter[343].[344]

This means that the Coroner must not only find the 'medical cause' of the death, but also the 'manner' of death, ie., the circumstances that resulted in the 'medical cause' of death.[345]

---

[340] See section 1(h) and Form 8 of the *Coroners Regulation* (Ch. 32).

[341] See section 299 of the *Criminal Code* (Ch. 262).

[342] See section 300 of the *Criminal Code* (Ch. 262).

[343] See section 301 of the *Criminal Code* (Ch. 262).

[344] See section 19 of the *Coroners Act* (Ch. 32).

Refer also to the section titled 'Homicide Offences' in the chapter titled 'Offences Against The Person' in the text titled 'Injia on Criminal Offences in Papua New Guinea and the Pacific'.

[345] See *Ex parte Minister of Justice; Re Malcolm* [1965] NSWR 1598.

FINDINGS

[3.2] NO DEATH

Where the Coroner finds that the person the subject of a coronial inquest has not died, the finding should state:

> 'I find on the balance of probabilities that the person AB, the subject of this coronial inquest, has not died.'

[3.3] DEATH UNCERTAIN

Where the Coroner is unable to find that the person, the subject of a coronial inquest died, the finding should state (for example):

> 'I find on the balance of probabilities that the human remains found on (date) at (location) were those of the deceased AB and that [he or she] died between (date) and (date).
>
> But as to the manner and cause of [his or her] death I am unable to make such a finding at this coronial inquest.'

[3.4] OPEN FINDING

An 'open finding' is appropriate where the evidence does not fully disclose the 'manner' of death.

FINDINGS

There are numerous cases where there may be a real doubt as to the 'manner' of death and where an 'open finding' is right, and where anything else is unjust to the family of the deceased.[346]

The following findings should be considered when a Coroner intends to make an 'open finding':

> 'I find on the balance of probabilities that on (date) at (location) the deceased AB, the subject of this coronial inquest, did die from [specify the 'medical cause' of death] **[medical cause]** as a consequence of the effects of [for example] self-ingested poisoning **[manner]**, but whether the deceased had the intention of taking [his or her] own life or otherwise, the evidence adduced does not enable me to say.'

> 'I find on the balance of probabilities that on (date) at (location) the deceased AB, the subject of this coronial inquest, did die from [specify the 'medical cause' of death] **[medical cause]** as a consequence of the effects of injuries suffered on (date) at (location) **[manner]**, but whether the deceased received those injuries accidentally or otherwise the evidence adduced does not enable me to say.'

> 'I find on the balance of probabilities that on (date) at (location) the deceased AB, the subject of this coronial inquest, did die from [specify the 'medical cause' of death] **[medical cause]** as a consequence of the effects of a medical condition namely [specify the medical condition] **[manner]**, but whether such a medical condition occurred accidentally or otherwise the evidence adduced does not enable me to say.'

346 See *R v Her Majesty's Coroner for the City of London; ex parte Barber* [1975] 3 All ER 538 at 540, [1975] 1 WLR 1325.

FINDINGS

[3.5] NATURAL CAUSES

When medical treatment does no more than fail to prevent death from a potentially fatal medical condition or natural cause, the appropriate conclusion is natural causes.[347]

When a deceased has died from natural causes, the finding should state:

> 'I find on the balance of probabilities that on (date) at (location) the deceased AB, the subject of this coronial inquest, did die from [specify the 'medical cause' of death] **[medical cause]** as a consequence of the effects of a natural cause **[manner]**, namely [specify the medical condition, such as for example] a heart attack.'

[3.6] SUICIDE[348]

Suicide is not to be presumed.[349]

A finding of suicide must be based on evidence of intention.[350]

---

[347] See *R v Her Majesty's Coroner for Birmingham and Sohihull; ex parte Benton* [1997] 8 Med LR 362 at 366.

See also: Halsbury's Laws of England, 4th edition, Volume 9(2), page 542.

[348] See also: sections 282 and 310 of the *Criminal Code* (Ch. 262).

[349] See *Re Davis, decd* [1968] 1 QB 72, per Sellers LJ.

See also: *R v Her Majesty's Coroner for the County of Surrey; ex parte Rosalind Ager* (Unrep. QBD, 24 May 1984) and *R v Huntbach; ex parte Lockley* [1944] 2 All ER 453.

[350] See Halsbury's Laws of England, 4th edition, Volume 9(2), page 544.

FINDINGS

If it is not proven by evidence that the deceased died by suicide then it is the duty of the Coroner to make an open finding.[351]

When a deceased has committed suicide, the finding should state:

Drug Overdose

> 'I find beyond reasonable doubt that on (date) at (location) the deceased AB, the subject of this coronial inquest, did die from [specify the 'medical cause' of death] **[medical cause]** as a consequence **[manner]** of the deceased killing [himself or herself] by [for example] the effects of poisoning by the consumption of chloroquine that was self-ingested and with the intention of taking [his or her] own life.'

Gassing

> 'I find beyond reasonable doubt that on (date) at (location) the deceased AB, the subject of this coronial inquest, did die from [specify the 'medical cause' of death] **[medical cause]** as a consequence of **[manner]** the deceased killing [himself or herself] by [for example] the effects of poisoning by carbon monoxide that was self-administered and with the intention of taking [his or her] own life.'

Shooting

> 'I find beyond reasonable doubt that on (date) at (location) the deceased AB, the subject of this coronial inquest, did die from [specify the 'medical cause' of death] **[medical cause]** as a consequence of **[manner]** the deceased killing [himself or herself] by [for example] the effect of a bullet wound to the head that was self-inflicted and with the intention of taking [his or her] own life.'

---

351 See *R v Her Majesty's Coroner for the City of London; ex parte Barber* [1975] 3 All ER 538, per Lord Widgery at 540, [1975] 1 WLR 1325.

FINDINGS

Hanging

'I find beyond reasonable doubt that on (date) at (location) the deceased AB, the subject of this coronial inquest, did die from [specify the 'medical cause' of death] **[medical cause]** as a consequence of **[manner]** the deceased killing [himself or herself] by [for example] wilfully hanging [himself or herself] and with the intention of taking [his or her] own life.'

Falling

'I find beyond reasonable doubt that on (date) at (location) the deceased AB, the subject of this coronial inquest, did die from [specify the 'medical cause' of death] **[medical cause]** as a consequence of **[manner]** the deceased killing [himself or herself] by [for example] the effects of multiple injuries sustained when the deceased jumped off a [specify from what the deceased did jump from, such as a cliff] and with the intention of taking [his or her] own life.'

Lacerations

'I find beyond reasonable doubt that on (date) at (location) the deceased AB, the subject of this coronial inquest, did die from [specify the 'medical cause' of death] **[medical cause]** as a consequence of **[manner]** the deceased killing [himself or herself] by [for example] the effects of blood loss resulting from incised wounds to the wrists that were self-inflicted and with the intention of taking [his or her] own life.'

[3.7] NEGLECT

'Lack of care', in the context of a coronial inquest[352] is the obverse of self-neglect and is more aptly described as 'neglect' which means:

> a gross failure to provide nourishment or liquid, or provide or procure basic medical attention or shelter or warmth for someone in a dependent position (because of youth, age, illness or incarceration) who cannot provide for himself or herself.[353]

However, there will generally be other reasons for the death, other than neglect.[354]

Lack of care only relates to the physical condition of a deceased as causing the death and should not be used to indicate a breach of duty by another.[355]

---

[352] See *Ex parte Hicks* [1987] 1 WLR 1624 at 1634; *R v Her Majesty's Coroner for Inner London North District; ex parte Linnane* [1989] 1 WLR 395 at 399, (1990) 155 JP 343, [1989] 2 All ER 254 and *Re Rapier, decd.* [1988] QB 26 at 37-38.

See also: Jervis on Coroners, 10th edition, pages 62-63.

[353] See *Her Majesty's Coroner for North Humberside and Scunthorpe; ex parte Jamieson* [1995] QB 1 at 25, (1994) 158 JP 1011.

See also: sections 283-285 and 323-325 of the *Criminal Code* (Ch. 262) and Halsbury's Laws of England, 4th edition, Volume 9(2), page 542.

[354] See *Her Majesty's Coroner for North Humberside and Scunthorpe; ex parte Jamieson* [1995] QB 1 at 25, (1994) 158 JP 1011.

See also: sections 283-285 and 323-325 of the *Criminal Code* (Ch. 262) and Halsbury's Laws of England, 4th edition, Volume 9(2), page 542.

[355] See *R v Southwark Coroner; ex parte Hicks* [1987] 1 WLR 1624 at 1632 and 1633-1634 and *R v Portsmouth Coroner; ex parte Anderson* [1987] 1 WLR 1640 at 1646-1648.

FINDINGS

When a deceased has died from neglect, the finding should state:

> 'I find on the balance of probabilities that on (date) at (location) the deceased AB, the subject of this coronial inquest, did die from [specify the 'medical cause' of death] **[medical cause]** as a consequence of **[manner]** a failure by CD to [provide (nourishment or liquid) or (procure or provide) (basic medical attention, shelter or warmth)] for the deceased who was dependent on that person and who could not provide for [himself or herself].'

[3.8] ACCIDENTAL DEATH

An 'accidental death' includes recreational hazards, industrial accidents, falls, drownings, burns, accidental gassing or poisonings, drug related deaths, aircraft accidents, suffocation and choking and electrocution.

An accidental death does not however occur as a consequence of a traffic accident.

It should be remembered that no death is purely 'accidental'.

Such deaths should be regarded as 'incidents' that are in most instances:

- preventable;

  and

- avoidable.

Therefore, a Coroner should avoid using the term 'accident', and use the term 'incident'.

FINDINGS

Appropriate recommendations and suitable comments made by a Coroner, when handing down findings, can assist in the prevention of future deaths in similar circumstances.

When a deceased dies as a consequence of an accidental death, the finding should state:

Industrial Accident

> 'I find on the balance of probabilities that on (date) at (location) the deceased AB, the subject of this coronial inquest, did die from [specify the 'medical cause' of death] **[medical cause]** as a consequence of **[manner]** the effects of injuries sustained [for example] by the deceased when the scaffolding that the deceased was on accidentally collapsed.'

Accidental Drowning

> 'I find on the balance of probabilities that on (date) at (location) the deceased AB, the subject of this coronial inquest, did die from [specify the 'medical cause' of death] **[medical cause]** as a consequence of **[manner]** the deceased accidentally drowning when [for example] fishing in the Buka Passage.'

Accidental Gassing

> 'I find on the balance of probabilities that on (date) at (location) the deceased AB, the subject of this coronial inquest, did die from [specify the 'medical cause' of death] **[medical cause]** as a consequence of **[manner]** [for example] the effects of poisoning by carbon monoxide inhaled when the mattress upon which the deceased was lying caught fire as a consequence of the deceased smoking in bed.'

FINDINGS

Accidental Fall

'I find on the balance of probabilities that on (date) at (location) the deceased AB, the subject of this coronial inquest, did die from [specify the 'medical cause' of death] **[medical cause]** as a consequence of **[manner]** the effects of injuries sustained by the deceased when the deceased did accidentally fall when [for example] the deceased was climbing a tree.'

Burns

'I find on the balance of probabilities that on (date) at (location) the deceased AB, the subject of this coronial inquest, did die from [specify the 'medical cause' of death] **[medical cause]** as a consequence of **[manner]** the effects of burns sustained by the deceased when [for example] the house of the deceased accidentally caught on fire.'

Suffocation and Choking

'I find on the balance of probabilities that on (date) at (location) the deceased AB, the subject of this coronial inquest, did die from [specify the 'medical cause' of death] **[medical cause]** as a consequence of **[manner]** asphyxia caused by [for example] the accidental inhalation of [his or her] stomach contents or food being accidentally caught in the throat of the deceased.'

Electrocution

'I find on the balance of probabilities that on (date) at (location) the deceased AB, the subject of this coronial inquest, did die from [specify the 'medical cause' of death] **[medical cause]** as a consequence **[manner]** of the deceased accidentally being electrocuted when the deceased [for example] put a steel knife through a live electrical wire.'

FINDINGS

[3.9] MISADVENTURE

[3.9.1] GENERALLY

A finding of 'misadventure' may be made in circumstances in which a person who is doing a lawful act and without the intention of injuring another person, accidentally kills another person.[356]

When a deceased dies as a consequence of misadventure generally, the finding should state:

> 'I find on the balance of probabilities that on (date) at (location) the deceased AB, the subject of this coronial inquest, did die from [specify the 'medical cause' of death] **[medical cause]** as a consequence **[manner]** of the effects of injuries sustained by the deceased when [for example] CD accidentally struck the deceased with a spear.'

[3.9.2] MEDICAL MISADVENTURE[357]

Where a person suffering from a non-life threatening medical condition dies as a consequence of medical treatment, and there is no question of unlawful killing, the appropriate conclusion is also 'misadventure'.[358]

---

[356] See Coronial Law and Practice in New South Wales, 3rd edition, page 87.

See also: sections 286-288 of the *Criminal Code* (Ch. 262).

[357] See Coronial Law and Practice in New South Wales, 3rd edition, page 189.

[358] See Halsbury's Laws of England, 4th edition, Volume 9(2), page 544.

See also: section 280 of the *Criminal Code* (Ch. 262).

FINDINGS

When a deceased dies as a consequence of medical misadventure, the finding should state:

> 'I find on the balance of probabilities that on (date) at (location) the deceased AB, the subject of this coronial inquest, who was suffering from [specify the 'medical cause' of death] **[medical cause]** did die as a consequence of **[manner]** the medical treatment administered for that condition.'

[3.10] TRAFFIC ACCIDENT[359]

When a deceased dies as a consequence of traffic accident, the finding should state:

> 'I find on the balance of probabilities that on (date) at (location) the deceased AB, the subject of this coronial inquest, did die from [specify the 'medical cause' of death] **[medical cause]** as a consequence of **[manner]** the effects of injuries sustained by the deceased in a traffic accident when [for example]

- the deceased was crossing (name) street and was struck by a motor vehicle driven by CD';
- the motor vehicle that was being driven by the deceased on (name) street collided with a tree';
- the deceased was a passenger in the motor vehicle on (name) street that was driven by CD when it collided with a motor vehicle driven by EF';
- the motor vehicle that the deceased was driving on (name) street collided with a motor vehicle being driven by CD'; and

---

[359] Refer also to sections 8 and 10 of the *Motor Vehicles (Third Party Insurance) (Basic Protection Compensation) Act* (Ch. 296).

- the deceased was a pillion passenger on a motor cycle that was being ridden on (name) street by CD when it collided with a motor vehicle being driven by EF.'

[3.11] KILLED UNLAWFULLY

The evidence needed to return a finding of unlawful killing is that needed to establish an unlawful homicide[360] which includes:

- 'Wilful Murder'[361];
- 'Murder'[362];
- 'Manslaughter'[363];

---

[360] See section 35 of the *Constitution of the Independent State of Papua New Guinea*.

[361] See section 299 of the *Criminal Code* (Ch. 262).

As regards the law in relation to the offence of 'Wilful Murder', refer to the section titled 'Homicide Offences' in the chapter titled 'Offences Against The Person' in the text titled 'Injia on Criminal Offences in Papua New Guinea and the Pacific'.

[362] See section 300 of the *Criminal Code* (Ch. 262).

As regards the law in relation to the offence of 'Murder', refer to the section titled 'Homicide Offences' in the chapter titled 'Offences Against The Person' in the text titled 'Injia on Criminal Offences in Papua New Guinea and the Pacific'.

[363] See section 301 of the *Criminal Code* (Ch. 262).

As regards the law in relation to the offence of 'Manslaughter', refer to the section titled 'Homicide Offences' in the chapter titled 'Offences Against The Person' in the text titled 'Injia on Criminal Offences in Papua New Guinea and the Pacific'.

- 'Infanticide'[364];

  and

- 'Dangerous Driving Causing Death'[365].[366]

A Coroner may make such a finding notwithstanding that the body of the deceased has not been located.[367]

In such a case the Coroner should specify that the finding of death was made notwithstanding that the body of the deceased has never been located.

---

[364] See section 302 of the *Criminal Code* (Ch. 262).

As regards the law in relation to the offence of 'Infanticide', refer to the section titled 'Homicide Offences' in the chapter titled 'Offences Against The Person' in the text titled 'Injia on Criminal Offences in Papua New Guinea and the Pacific'.

[365] See section 328(5) of the *Criminal Code* (Ch. 262).

As regards the law in relation to the offence of 'Dangerous Driving Causing Death', refer to the chapter titled 'Traffic Offences' in the text titled 'Injia on Criminal Offences in Papua New Guinea and the Pacific'.

[366] See Halsbury's Laws of England, 4th edition, Volume 9(2), page 546.

See also: sections 281, 283-289 and 298 of the *Criminal Code* (Ch. 262).

[367] See *R v Burdett* (1820) 4 B & Ald 95, 106 ER 873; *R v Makin* (1893) 14 LR (NSW) 1 and *R v Onufrejczyk* [1955] 1 QB 388.

See also: *Roberts v The State of Western Australia* [2007] WASCA 48; *Macartney v R* (2006) 31 WAR 416 at 438-455, [2006] WASCA 29; *R v Horry* [1952] NZLR 111; *Attorney-General's Reference No. 6 of 1980* (1981) 73 Cr App R 40, [1981] 3 WLR 125, [1981] 2 All ER 1057, [1981] QB 715, [1981] Crim LR 533; *R v Rice* [1996] 2 VR 406, per Brooking JA at 412; *Peacock v R* (1911) 13 CLR 619; *R v Ryan* [1906] St R Qd 15; *Weissensteiner v R* (1993) 178 CLR 217; *Burrell v R* [2007] NSWCCA 65 and *Burrell v R* [2009] NSWCCA 193.

FINDINGS

When a deceased dies as a consequence of being killed unlawfully, the finding should state:

> 'I find on the balance of probabilities that on (date) at (location) the deceased AB, the subject of this coronial inquest, did die from [specify the 'medical cause' of death] **[medical cause]** as a consequence of **[manner]** being unlawfully killed by CD and in such circumstances CD should be charged with the offence of [Wilful Murder, Murder, Manslaughter, Infanticide or Dangerous Driving Causing Death].'

A Coroner may however only commit a person for trial or sentence in relation to the offences of Wilful Murder, Murder and Manslaughter.[368]

A Coroner must follow the statutory procedures as specified in the *Coroners Act* (Ch. 32) when committing a person for trial or sentence in the National Court.[369]

A Coroner should forward a copy of the investigation file together with his or her findings to the Commissioner of Police, Royal Papua New Guinea Constabulary/Chief of Police, Bougainville Police Service when:

- he or she is satisfied that a person has committed the offences of Infanticide or Dangerous Driving Causing Death;

  or

---

[368] See section 19 of the *Coroners Act* (Ch. 32).

See also: sections 10(b)(iii), 22, 23(3) and 27(b) of the *Coroners Act* (Ch. 32) and sections 1(d) and 1(g) and Forms 4 and 7 of the *Coroners Regulation* (Ch. 32).

[369] See *Sakawar Kasieng v Andrew Baigry, Magistrate of Wewak District Court and The State* (2004) N2562.

As regards the application of section 23(3) of the *Coroners Act* (Ch. 32) to the National Court, see *The State v Samson Wailo (No. 2)* [1991] PNGLR 150.

- a person to be committed as provided for by section 19 of the *Coroners Act* (Ch. 32) is not at the coronial inquest.

The police must then institute proceedings following normal procedures.[370]

[3.12] KILLED LAWFULLY[371]

[3.12.1] CONSTITUTIONAL PROVISIONS

Section 35 of the *Constitution of the Independent State of Papua New Guinea* states:

'(1) No person shall be deprived of his life intentionally except--

(a) in execution of a sentence of a court following his conviction of an offence for which the penalty of death is prescribed by law; or

(b) as the result of the use of force to such an extent as is reasonable in the circumstances of the case and is permitted by any other law--

(i) for the defence of any person from violence; or

(ii) in order to effect a lawful arrest or to prevent the escape of a person lawfully detained; or

(iii) for the purpose of suppressing a riot, an insurrection or a mutiny; or

(iv) in order to prevent him from committing an offence; or

---

[370] As regards the law in relation to 'Institution Of Proceedings', refer to the chapter titled 'Charges' in the text titled 'Injia on Criminal Practice and Procedure in Papua New Guinea and the Pacific'.

[371] Refer also to the chapter titled 'Police Powers' in the text titled 'Injia on Investigatory Practice in Papua New Guinea and the Pacific'.

(v) for the purpose of suppressing piracy or terrorism or similar acts[372]; or

(c) as the result of a lawful act of war.

(2) Nothing in Subsection (1)(b) relieves any person from any liability at law in respect of the killing of another'.

Section 41 states:

'(1) Notwithstanding anything to the contrary in any other provision of any law, any act that is done under a valid law but in the particular case--

(a) is harsh or oppressive; or

(b) is not warranted by, or is disproportionate to, the requirements of the particular circumstances or of the particular case; or

(c) is otherwise not, in the particular circumstances, reasonably justifiable in a democratic society having a proper regard for the rights and dignity of mankind,
is a lawful act.

(2) The burden of showing that Subsection (1)(a), (b) or (c) applies in respect of an act is on the party alleging it, and may be discharged on the balance of probabilities.

(3) Nothing in this section affects the operation of any other law under which an act may be held to be unlawful or invalid'.

---

[372] There is no statutory provision that relates specifically to the suppression of piracy, terrorism or similar acts.

See Division 1 of Part V of the *Criminal Code* (Ch. 262).

FINDINGS

[3.12.2] ACTING IN SELF DEFENCE

A police officer may use force to such an extent as is:

- 'reasonable' in the circumstances of the case;

  and

- permitted by any other law

for the defence of any person from violence.[373]

In relation to any person, including a police officer, acting in self defence of any person from violence, ie., acting in self-defence, lethal force may be used:

- subject to sections 269, 270 and 271 of the *Criminal Code* (Ch. 262)[374];

  and

- provided that the force used is reasonable in the circumstances of the case[375].

An officer is justified in using lethal force, including the use of a firearm, provided that the officer believes on reasonable grounds that there is no other option in defending himself or herself or any other person from death or suffering grievous bodily harm.[376]

---

[373] See section 35(1)(b)(i) of the *Constitution of the Independent State of Papua New Guinea*.

[374] Refer also to the section titled 'Defences' in the chapter titled 'Offences Against The Person' in the text titled 'Injia on Criminal Offences in Papua New Guinea and the Pacific'.

[375] See section 35(1)(b) of the *Constitution of the Independent State of Papua New Guinea.*

[376] See also: International Human Rights Instruments titled 'Basic Principles on the Use of Force and Firearms by Law Enforcement Officials' and 'Basic Principles on the Use of Force and Firearms by Law Enforcement Officials'.

However, lethal force should always be the option of last resort.

[3.12.3] EFFECT AN ARREST

A police officer may use force to such an extent as is:

- 'reasonable' in the circumstances of the case;

  and

- permitted by any other law

in order to effect a lawful arrest.[377]

Section 14 of the *Arrest Act* (Ch. 339) states (in part):

> '(1) Where an authorised person intends to make an arrest and the person to be arrested--
>
> (c) resists the arrest, whether by force or by refusing to move [...] the authorised person may, subject to Subsection (2), use all reasonable means to make the arrest.
>
> (2) Subsection (1)(c) does not justify the use of greater force than is reasonable in the circumstances'.

[377] See section 35(1)(b)(ii) of the *Constitution of the Independent State of Papua New Guinea*.

Refer also to the chapter titled 'Police Powers' in the text titled 'Injia on Investigatory Practice in Papua New Guinea and the Pacific'.

FINDINGS

[3.12.4] PREVENT AN ESCAPE

A police officer may use force to such an extent as is:

- 'reasonable' in the circumstances of the case;

  and

- permitted by any other law

in order to prevent the escape of a person lawfully detained.[378]

Section 14 of the *Arrest Act* (Ch. 339) states (in part):

> '(1) Where an authorised person intends to make an arrest and the person to be arrested--
>
> (c) [...] seeks to evade arrest, whether by running away or by other means, the authorised person may, subject to Subsection (2), use all reasonable means to make the arrest.
>
> (2) Subsection (1)(c) does not justify the use of greater force than is reasonable in the circumstances'.

[378] See section 35(1)(b)(ii) of the *Constitution of the Independent State of Papua New Guinea*.

Refer also to the chapter titled 'Police Powers' in the text titled 'Injia on Investigatory Practice in Papua New Guinea and the Pacific'.

FINDINGS

[3.12.5] SUPPRESS A RIOT, INSURRECTION OR MUTINY

A police officer may use force to such an extent as is:

- 'reasonable' in the circumstances of the case;

  and

- permitted by any other law

for the purpose of suppressing a riot, an insurrection or a mutiny.[379]

Section 259 of the *Criminal Code* (Ch. 262) states:

'It is lawful for any person to use such force as is--

(a) necessary to suppress a riot; and

(b) reasonably proportioned to the danger to be apprehended from its continuance'.

Section 260 states:

'It is lawful for a magistrate to use, or order to be used, and for a member of the Police Force to use, such force as--

(a) he believes, on reasonable grounds, to be necessary in order to suppress a riot; and

(b) is reasonably proportioned to the danger that he believes, on reasonable grounds, is to be apprehended from its continuance'.

---

[379] See section 35(1)(b)(iii) of the *Constitution of the Independent State of Papua New Guinea*.

Refer also to the chapter titled 'Police Powers' in the text titled 'Injia on Investigatory Practice in Papua New Guinea and the Pacific'.

Those statutory provisions however do not relate to the suppression of an insurrection or a mutiny.

[3.12.6] PREVENTING AN ESCAPE

A police officer may use force to such an extent as is:

- 'reasonable' in the circumstances of the case;

  and

- permitted by any other law

in order to prevent an offender from committing an offence.[380]

Section 264 of the *Criminal Code* (Ch. 262) states (in part):

> 'It is lawful for any person to use such force as is reasonably necessary in order to prevent--
>
> (a) the commission of an offence other than an offence specified by law (including this Code) to be an offence for which a person may only be arrested by virtue of a warrant; or
>
> (b) any act from being done that he believes, on reasonable grounds, would amount to such an offence'.

[380] See section 35(1)(b)(iv) of the *Constitution of the Independent State of Papua New Guinea*.

Refer also to the chapter titled 'Police Powers' in the text titled 'Injia on Investigatory Practice in Papua New Guinea and the Pacific'.

FINDINGS

An officer who intentionally shoots a person in order to prevent him or her from escaping and in doing so causes that person's death is guilty of the offence of 'Murder'.[381]

[3.12.7] WORDING

When a deceased dies as a consequence of being killed lawfully, the finding should state:

> 'I find on the balance of probabilities that on (date) at (location) the deceased AB, the subject of this coronial inquest, did die from [specify the 'medical cause' of death] **[medical cause]** as a consequence of **[manner]** the effects of [specify the injury] sustained when [specify how the deceased suffered the injury, for example, CD shot him or her in the chest] and the use of such force was reasonable in the circumstances
>
> - for the defence of a person namely [...] from violence;
> - in order to effect [a lawful arrest or to prevent the escape] of a person lawfully detained namely [...];
> - for the purpose of [suppressing a riot, an insurrection or a mutiny]';
> - in order to prevent the deceased from committing an offence to wit [specify the offence];
> - for the purpose of suppressing [piracy. terrorism or similar acts to wit [specify the similar acts]; or
> - as the result of a lawful act of war'.

---

[381] See *The State v John Kule* (2009) N3619.

See also: section 35(1)(b)(ii) of the *Constitution of the Independent State of Papua New Guinea*.

Refer also to the section titled 'Homicide Offences' in the chapter titled 'Offences Against The Person' in the text titled 'Injia on Criminal Offences in Papua New Guinea and the Pacific'.

FINDINGS

[4.0] FIRE INQUEST

The Coroner shall after hearing the evidence give his or her decision or finding and certify it in writing in the prescribed form[382] stating:

- the time when and the place where the fire occurred[383];

- the 'cause' of the fire;

  and

- where the offence of 'Arson'[384] has been committed, the person (if any) whom the Coroner finds to have been guilty of the offence.[385]

---

[382] See section 1(h) and Form 8 of the *Coroners Regulation* (Ch. 32).

[383] ie., its 'origin'.

[384] See section 436 of the *Criminal Code* (Ch. 262).

As regards the law in relation to the offence of 'Arson', refer also to the chapter titled 'Offences Against Property' in the text titled 'Injia on Criminal Offences in Papua New Guinea and the Pacific'.

[385] See section 17(4) of the *Coroners Act* (Ch. 32).

FINDINGS

Depending on the circumstances of the fire, the finding should state:

> 'I find on the balance of probabilities that on (date) at (location) property to wit [specify the property] the property of [specify the name/s of the owner/s] the subject of this coronial inquest was [destroyed or damaged] by fire that originated in [specify location] **[origin]** and was set by **[cause]** [CD or a person or persons unknown] [accidentally or intentionally and in such circumstances that person should be charged with the offence of Arson].'

> 'I find on the balance of probabilities that on (date) at (location) property to wit [specify the properly] the property of [specify the name/s of the owner/s] the subject of this coronial inquest was [destroyed or damaged] by fire which originated in [specify location] **[origin]** and was caused by **[cause]** an [electrical fault].'

A Coroner may only commit a person for trial or sentence in relation to the offence of Arson.[386]

A Coroner must follow the statutory procedures as specified in the *Coroners Act* (Ch. 32) when committing a person for trial or sentence in the National Court.[387]

A Coroner should forward a copy of the investigation file together with his or her findings to the Commissioner of Police, Royal Papua New Guinea Constabulary/Chief of Police, Bougainville Police Service when the person to be committed is not at the coronial inquest.

---

[386] See section 19 of the *Coroners Act* (Ch. 32).

See also: sections 10(b)(iii), 22, 23(3) and 27(b) of the *Coroners Act* (Ch. 32) and sections 1(d) and 1(g) and Forms 4 and 7 of the *Coroners Regulation* (Ch. 32).

[387] See *Sakawar Kasieng v Andrew Baigry, Magistrate of Wewak District Court and The State* (2004) N2562.

As regards the application of section 23(3) of the *Coroners Act* (Ch. 32) to the National Court, see *The State v Samson Wailo (No. 2)* [1991] PNGLR 150.

The police must then institute proceedings following normal procedures.[388]

[5.0] MISSING PERSON INQUEST

After hearing the evidence the Coroner shall:

- give his or her decision or finding in writing signed by him or her[389];

  and

- forward the decision or finding to the Attorney-General together with the depositions.[390]

The Coroner may also make a finding that a specified person did cause the death of a missing person by the commission of the offence of:

- 'Wilful Murder'[391];
- 'Murder'[392];

[388] As regards the law in relation to 'Institution Of Proceedings', refer to the chapter titled 'Charges' in the text titled 'Injia on Criminal Practice and Procedure in Papua New Guinea and the Pacific'.

[389] See section 1(h) and Form 8 of the *Coroners Regulation* (Ch. 32).

[390] See section 20(4) of the *Coroners Act* (Ch. 32).

[391] See section 299 of the *Criminal Code* (Ch. 262).

As regards the law in relation to the offence of 'Wilful Murder', refer to the section titled 'Homicide Offences' in the chapter titled 'Offences Against The Person' in the text titled 'Injia on Criminal Offences in Papua New Guinea and the Pacific'.

[392] See section 300 of the *Criminal Code* (Ch. 262).

As regards the law in relation to the offence of 'Murder', refer to the section titled 'Homicide Offences' in the chapter titled 'Offences Against The Person' in the text titled 'Injia on Criminal Offences in Papua New Guinea and the Pacific'.

or

- 'Manslaughter'[393].[394]

A Coroner may make such a finding notwithstanding that the body of the missing person has not been located.[395]

Depending on the circumstances of the missing person, the finding should state:

> 'I find on the balance of probabilities that the cause and circumstances of the disappearance of the missing person, AB of [last known permanent place of residence], [aged … years or of an approximate age of … years] are as follows
>
> - the date that the missing person was last seen was …;
>
> - the place that the missing person was last seen was …; and

---

[393] See section 301 of the *Criminal Code* (Ch. 262).

As regards the law in relation to the offence of 'Manslaughter', refer to the section titled 'Homicide Offences' in the chapter titled 'Offences Against The Person' in the text titled 'Injia on Criminal Offences in Papua New Guinea and the Pacific'.

[394] See *The State v John Kule* (2009) N3619.

See also: section 35(1)(b)(ii) of the *Constitution of the Independent State of Papua New Guinea*.

[395] See *R v Burdett* (1820) 4 B & Ald 95, 106 ER 873; *R v Makin* (1893) 14 LR (NSW) 1 and *R v Onufrejczyk* [1955] 1 QB 388.

See also: *Roberts v The State of Western Australia* [2007] WASCA 48; *Macartney v R* (2006) 31 WAR 416 at 438-455, [2006] WASCA 29; *R v Horry* [1952] NZLR 111; *Attorney-General's Reference No. 6 of 1980* (1981) 73 Cr App R 40, [1981] 3 WLR 125, [1981] 2 All ER 1057, [1981] QB 715, [1981] Crim LR 533; *R v Rice* [1996] 2 VR 406, per Brooking JA at 412; *Peacock v R* (1911) 13 CLR 619; *R v Ryan* [1906] St R Qd 15; *Weissensteiner v R* (1993) 178 CLR 217; *Burrell v R* [2007] NSWCCA 65 and *Burrell v R* [2009] NSWCCA 193.

- briefly specify the circumstances leading up to the disappearance of the missing person.

I am [able or unable] to make a finding as to whether the missing person is currently [alive or likely to be alive].

I find that the missing person is [alive or dead].

I am [able or unable] to make a finding as to current whereabouts of the missing person.

I find that the missing person is currently at ...'

When a Coroner is satisfied that a missing person has been unlawfully killed, the finding should also state:

> 'I find on the balance of probabilities that the missing person did die from [specify the 'medical cause' of death] **[medical cause]** as a consequence of **[manner]** being unlawfully killed by CD and in such circumstances CD should be charged with the offence of [Wilful Murder, Murder, Manslaughter, Infanticide or Dangerous Driving Causing Death].'

A Coroner may however only commit a person for trial or sentence in relation to the offences of:

- 'Wilful Murder'[396];

- 'Murder'[397];

---

396 See section 299 of the *Criminal Code* (Ch. 262).

As regards the law in relation to the offence of 'Wilful Murder', refer to the section titled 'Homicide Offences' in the chapter titled 'Offences Against The Person' in the text titled 'Injia on Criminal Offences in Papua New Guinea and the Pacific'.

397 See section 300 of the *Criminal Code* (Ch. 262).

As regards the law in relation to the offence of 'Murder', refer to the section titled 'Homicide Offences' in the chapter titled 'Offences Against The Person' in the text titled 'Injia on Criminal Offences in Papua New Guinea and the Pacific'.

or

- 'Manslaughter'[398].[399]

A Coroner must follow the statutory procedures as specified in the *Coroners Act* (Ch. 32) when committing a person for trial or sentence in the National Court.[400]

A Coroner should forward a copy of the investigation file together with his or her findings to the Commissioner of Police, Royal Papua New Guinea Constabulary/Chief of Police, Bougainville Police Service when:

- he or she is satisfied that a person has committed the offences of 'Infanticide' or 'Dangerous Driving Causing Death';

  or

- the person to be committed as provided for by section 19 of the *Coroners Act* (Ch. 32) is not at the coronial inquest.

The police must then institute proceedings following normal procedures.[401]

---

[398] See section 301 of the *Criminal Code* (Ch. 262).

As regards the law in relation to the offence of 'Manslaughter', refer to the section titled 'Homicide Offences' in the chapter titled 'Offences Against The Person' in the text titled 'Injia on Criminal Offences in Papua New Guinea and the Pacific'.

[399] See *The State v John Kule* (2009) N3619.

See also: section 35(1)(b)(ii) of the *Constitution of the Independent State of Papua New Guinea*.

[400] See *Sakawar Kasieng v Andrew Baigry, Magistrate of Wewak District Court and The State* (2004) N2562.

As regards the application of section 23(3) of the *Coroners Act* (Ch. 32) to the National Court, see *The State v Samson Wailo (No. 2)* [1991] PNGLR 150.

[401] As regards the law in relation to 'Institution Of Proceedings', refer to the chapter titled 'Charges' in the text titled 'Injia on Criminal Practice and Procedure in Papua New Guinea and the Pacific'.

COMMENTS AND/OR RECOMMENDATIONS

[1.0] GENERALLY

Apart from making his or her findings, the Coroner may also provide comments and/or recommendations as to how:

- the death;

  or

- the fire

could have been prevented based on the evidence, although such comments or recommendations are not part of the findings of the Coroner[402].

Adverse comments however may be quashed by the National Court, unless based on the evidence.[403]

A Coroner may also make a comment and recommendation even though a coronial inquest has not been held.

Comments and recommendations are usually directed at:

- a government department;
- a private organisation;

---

[402] See *X v Deputy State Coroner for New South Wales* (2001) 51 NSWLR 312, [2001] NSWSC 46.

[403] See *S v The Director of Public Prosecutions and others* [2007] ACTSC 100 and *McGregor and Pearce v The Honorable John Gallop and the Attorney-General of the Australian Capital Territory* [2002] ACTSC 45.

or

- an individual

in order to try to avoid a similar death or fire from occurring.

But a recommendation has no legal basis and at common law may be accepted or rejected at will by the person asked to consider it.[404]

[2.0] DEATH INQUESTS SPECIFICALLY

An important objective of a coronial inquest in relation to a death is to enable the Coroner to make comments and/or recommendations in relation to:

- avoiding circumstances similar to those in which the death occurred;

  or

- how people should act in circumstances similar to those in which the death occurred in order to reduce the chances of similar deaths occurring.[405]

[404] See *Director of National Parks and Wildlife v Dennis Joseph Barritt SM, a Coroner for the Northern Territory of Australia and Attorney-General for the Northern Territory of Australia* (1990) 72 NTR 1, [1990] NTSC 37.

[405] See New Zealand Law Commission, 1999, 'Coroner A Review A Discussion Paper', Preliminary Paper 36, page 2 and New Zealand Law Commission, 2000, 'Coroners', Report 62, page 3.

COMMENTS AND/OR RECOMMENDATIONS

The social and preventative function of a coronial inquest which focuses on the public interest has become, in some cases, just as important as the distinctly separate function of investigating the individual facts of individual deaths.[406]

---

[406] See *People First of Ontario v Porter, Regional Coroner Niagara* (1991) 5 OR (3d) 609, (1991) 85 DLR (4th) 174; sub nom *People First of Ontario v Niagara (Regional Coroner)* at 617 and 182 [reversed on other grounds (1992) 6 OR (3d) 289, (1992) 87 DLR (4th) 765].

See also: Ontario Law Reform Commission, 1995, 'Report on the Law of Coroners', page 148.

EXHIBITS

Every exhibit at a coronial inquest should, unless the Coroner otherwise directs, be retained by him or her until the Coroner is satisfied that the exhibit:

- is not likely to be:

  or

- will no longer be

required for the purposes of any other legal proceedings.[407]

[407] See Halsbury's Laws of England, 4th edition, Volume 9(2), page 552.

CONTEMPT OF COURT

When a person:

- insults the Coroner during the holding of a coronial inquest;
- wilfully interrupts the proceedings at a coronial inquest;
- obstructs a person in attendance at a coronial inquest;
- assaults a person in attendance at a coronial inquest;
- refuses to obey a lawful order of the Coroner;

  or

- neglects to obey a lawful order of the Coroner,

the Coroner may impose on that person a fine not exceeding K40.[408]

---

[408] See section 28 of the *Coroners Act* (Ch. 32).

See also: section 1(e) and Form 5 of the *Coroners Regulation* (Ch. 32).

Refer also to the chapter titled 'Contempt Of Court' in the text titled 'Injia on Criminal Practice and Procedure in Papua New Guinea and the Pacific'.

RE-OPENING

When the Attorney-General directs a Coroner to re-open a coronial inquest, the Coroner shall re-open the inquest closed by him or her or another Coroner.[409]

A Coroner may re-open a coronial inquest when:

- he or she is of the opinion that a coronial inquest ought to be re-opened;

  or

- the Commissioner of Police, a Superintendent of Police or the husband, wife, father, mother, sister, brother, son, daughter or guardian of a deceased[410] requests him or her to re-open a coronial inquest.[411]

  Before re-opening a coronial inquest at the request of such a person a Coroner may require a written statement of the grounds for the request.[412]

  Where the Coroner considers that such grounds do not warrant the re-opening of a coronial inquest he or she:

  - may refuse to re-open the coronial inquest;

    and

  - shall in writing accompanied by a copy of the grounds for his or her refusal inform the Attorney-General as to his or her refusal.[413]

---

[409] See section 21(1)(a) of the *Coroners Act* (Ch. 32).

[410] See section 21(5) of the *Coroners Act* (Ch. 32).

[411] See section 21(2) of the *Coroners Act* (Ch. 32).

[412] See section 21(3) of the *Coroners Act* (Ch. 32).

[413] See section 21(4) of the *Coroners Act* (Ch. 32).

JUDICIAL REVIEW

Even though there is no right of appeal[414], there is still the right of review whereby an interested party may apply to the National Court to make orders in the nature of prerogative writs and such other orders as are necessary to do justice in the circumstances of the particular case.[415]

However, a Coroner is faced with a very difficult task and must be afforded a sufficient degree of insulation from review.[416]

A Coroner must have the power to:

- keep the coronial inquest from turning into a circus;

  and

- prevent every busybody from using the inquest as a platform for their particular views.[417]

---

[414] The fundamental right to appeal a decision of a court is a creature of statute [see for example, the *Supreme Court Act* (Ch. 37), *Supreme Court Rules 1984* and *District Courts Act* (Ch. 40)], but that right only exists to the extent created by statute [see *Kiau Nikints v Moki Rumints* [1990] PNGLR 123; *Kimbe Bakery Pty Ltd v Ben Jalatang* (1993) N1274 and *Chief Collector of Taxes v Bougainville Copper Limited* (2008) SC920, [2008] PGSC 13].

There is however no statutory provision in the *Coroners Act* (Ch. 32) that provides for an appeal of the decision of a Coroners Court.

[415] See section 155(4) of the *Constitution of the Independent State of Papua New Guinea*.

See also: *Ex parte Rutledge* (1943) 60 WN (NSW) 184 and *R v Ian Roger Matterson; ex parte Christine Debra Moles* [1994] 4 Tas R 87.

[416] See *Stanford v Regional Coroner, Eastern Ontario* (1989) 38 CPC (2d) 161, 38 Admin LR 141 at 172-74.

[417] See *Stanford v Regional Coroner, Eastern Ontario* (1989) 38 CPC (2d) 161, 38 Admin LR 141 at 172-74.

JUDICIAL REVIEW

Applications for judicial review should be discouraged as such applications detract from the Coroner's ability to control the proceedings and produce delay.[418]

The reasons given by a Coroner should not be scrutinized upon by over-zealous judicial review intent on discerning whether some inadequacy may be gleaned from the way in which the reasons are expressed.[419]

The constitutional basis for holding a judicial review by the National Court is section 155(3) of the *Constitution of the Independent State of Papua New Guinea*.

In determining whether there should be a judicial review is an exercise of judicial discretion.[420]

In an application for leave to apply for judicial review involving a coronial inquest the following criteria need to be satisfied in order for a Court to exercise its discretion in favour of the application:

- that it is in the interests of justice to grant leave;
- there are cogent and convincing reasons and exceptional circumstances, eg., some substantial injustice is manifest or the case is of special gravity;

  and

- there are clear legal grounds meriting a review.[421]

---

[418] See *Stanford v Regional Coroner, Eastern Ontario* (1989) 38 CPC (2d) 161, 38 Admin LR 141 at 172-74.

[419] See *Minister for Immigration and Ethnic Affairs v Wu Shan Liang* (1996) 185 CR 259 at 272, [1996] HCA 6 and *Doomadgee v Clements* [2006] 2 Qd R 352 at 360, [2005] QSC 357.

[420] See *NTN Pty Ltd v Board of Post and Telecommunication Corporation and others* [1987] PNGLR 70, per Wilson J at 74.

[421] See *Tay v Gerau* (2011) SC1097, [2011] PGSC 10.

JUDICIAL REVIEW

The purpose of judicial review by the National Court is not to examine the reasoning of the Coroners Court with a view to substituting its own opinion.[422]

Judicial review is concerned not with the decision, but the decision-making process.[423]

Judicial review is not just about procedural fairness, but it does under section 155(4) of the *Constitution of the Independent State of Papua New Guinea* empower the Court to make orders that are necessary to do justice in a particular case.[424]

In any judicial review the Court's determination of the review proceeds in the following stages:

- determining whether the plaintiff has proven one or more grounds of review;

and if it has

- deciding as a matter of discretion what remedies, if any, should be granted.[425]

---

[422] See *Moi Avei and Electoral Commission v Charles Maino* (1998) SC584, [1998] PGSC 45 and *Kekedo v Burns Philip and others* [1988-89] PNGLR 122.

See also: *Associated Provincial Pictures House Ltd v Wednesbury Corporation* [1948] 1 KB 223, [1947] 2 All ER 680.

[423] See *Moi Avei and Electoral Commission v Charles Maino* (1998) SC584, [1998] PGSC 45 and *Kekedo v Burns Philip and others* [1988-89] PNGLR 122.

See also: *Associated Provincial Pictures House Ltd v Wednesbury Corporation* [1948] 1 KB 223, [1947] 2 All ER 680.

[424] See *Kathy Dob v The Commissioner for Police and the State* (1998) OS 522 of 1996.

[425] See *Dale Christopher Smith v Minister for Lands* (2009) SC973; *Madang Cocoa Growers Export Co Ltd v Tautea* (2012) N4584, [2012] PGNC 5 and *Isaac Lupari v Sir Michael Somare* (2008) N3476.

JUDICIAL REVIEW

A long delay between:

- the conclusion of a coronial inquest;

  and

- the release of the findings, recommendations and comments

may warrant close scrutiny.[426]

Where:

- an error of law has been established[427];
- the Coroners Court exceeds or acts without jurisdiction[428];
- the Coroner misconducted himself or herself[429];
- there are defects apparent on the face of the coronial inquiry[430];

---

[426] See *Expectation Pty Ltd v PRD Realty Pty Ltd* (2004) 140 FCR 17 at 32, [2004] FCAFC 189; *Hadid v Redpath* [2001] NSWCA 416; *A Team Diamond Headquarters Pty Ltd v Main Road Property Group Pty Ltd* [2009] VSCA 208 and *Cahir v Jamieson and others* [2010] VSC 285.

[427] See *Moi Avei and Electoral Commission v Charles Maino* (1998) SC584, [1998] PGSC 45.

See also: *Associated Provincial Picture Houses Ltd v Wednesbury Corporation* [1948] 1 KB 223, [1947] 2 All ER 680.

[428] See *Moi Avei and Electoral Commission v Charles Maino* (1998) SC584, [1998] PGSC 45; *Sakawar Kasieng v Andrew Baigry, Magistrate of Wewak District Court and The State* (2004) N2562 and *Robert Lak v Daisy (Dessie) Magaru (Presiding Magistrate at Waigani District Court (Grade V) Committal Court and The State* (2000) N1956.

See also: *Ex Parte Rutledge* (1943) 60 WN (NSW) 184, per Jordan CJ.

[429] See *Ex Parte Rutledge* (1943) 60 WN (NSW) 184, per Jordan CJ.

[430] See *Ex Parte Rutledge* (1943) 60 WN (NSW) 184, per Jordan CJ.

- the Coroner took into account irrelevant considerations[431];
- the Coroner did fail to take into account relevant considerations[432];
- there appears that insufficient inquiry was made[433];
- a finding had been reached that was so unreasonable or absurd when having regard to all of the facts[434];
- there has been an incorrect determination on standing[435];
- there has been procedural irregularity[436];
- the Coroner makes a determination that he or she was not authorised to make[437];
- when it is plain that the decision reached is such as to be unsustainable in law or reason[438];

---

[431] See *Associated Provincial Picture Houses Ltd v Wednesbury Corporation* [1948] 1 KB 223, [1947] 2 All ER 680.

[432] See *Associated Provincial Picture Houses Ltd v Wednesbury Corporation* [1948] 1 KB 223, [1947] 2 All ER 680.

[433] See *Ex Parte Rutledge* (1943) 60 WN (NSW) 184, per Jordan CJ.

[434] See *Madang Cocoa Growers Export Co Ltd v Tautea* (2012) N4584, [2012] PGNC 5; *Paul Saboko v Commissioner of Police* (2006) N2975 and *Dopsie v Tetaga and Apeng* (2009) N3722.

See also: *Associated Provincial Picture Houses Ltd v Wednesbury Corporation* [1948] 1 KB 223, [1947] 2 All ER 680.

[435] See *Stanford v Regional Coroner, Eastern Ontario* (1989) 38 CPC (2d) 161, 38 Admin LR 141 at 172-174.

[436] See *Moi Avei and Electoral Commission v Charles Maino* (1998) SC584, [1998] PGSC 45.

[437] See *Moi Avei and Electoral Commission v Charles Maino* (1998) SC584, [1998] PGSC 45.

[438] See *Moi Avei and Electoral Commission v Charles Maino* (1998) SC584, [1998] PGSC 45.

or

- facts have come to light since the coronial inquest that make a further inquest desirable[439]

then it would be appropriate for the National Court to intervene by way of judicial review.

In some cases:

- an assessment of the cogency of the evidence in support of an application for a new coronial inquest;

  and

- the extent to which it alters conclusions reached in the earlier inquest,

are seen as matter for a second inquest, rather than for final determination by the Court.[440]

However, judicial review is not a readily available remedy for a review of the decision of a Coroners Court to commit a person to stand trial before the National Court.[441]

---

439 See *Ex Parte Rutledge* (1943) 60 WN (NSW) 184, per Jordan CJ.

440 See *Re Rapier* [1988] QB 26 at 34.

441 See *Sakawar Kasieng v Andrew Baigry, Magistrate of Wewak District Court and The State* (2004) N2562.

GLOSSARY OF MEDICAL TERMS

A

Abdomen	Part of the body which lies below the chest and above the pelvis. It contains the liver, stomach and most of the digestive system.
Abrasion	A wound caused by rubbing or scraping of the skin (scratch).
Alimentary	Pertaining to or caused by food or nutritive material.
Anthrax	A boil (carbuncle) or other infections caused by the anthrax bacteria.
Aorta	The major blood vessel that carries blood from the heart to the rest of the body.
Aperture	An opening (orifice).
Articular	Pertaining to a joint, eg., knee or elbow.

GLOSSARY OF MEDICAL TERMS

Asphyxiation	A state in which the body lacks oxygen for utilization by tissues and there is an increase in carbon dioxide in the blood. (suffocation)
Atherosclerosis	A condition in which there are deposits of cholesterol plaques in walls of arteries (blood vessels) causing hardening of the walls.
Atrium	One of the pair of smaller chambers with thin musculature consisting of the upper part of the heart in which the blood follows to the ventricles. (lower chambers)
Artery	A blood vessel through which the blood passes away from the heart to various parts of the body carrying oxygen and nutrients.
Autopsy	Examination of a body after death in order to determine the actual cause of death. (Also referred to as a post-mortem examination or necroscopy.)

GLOSSARY OF MEDICAL TERMS

B

Basal Fracture	Break in the continuity of a bone at the base of the skull.
Bile Duct	The canals that conduct bile, a greenish fluid produced by the liver to the small intestine.
Bladder	A membranous sac situated behind and above the public bone (front of pelvis) where urine is stored until it leaves the body. (Also referred to as urinary bladder.)
Bowel	Passage way in which digested food passes from the stomach to the anus.
Bronchi	The large passages conveying air to and within the lungs.
Bruise	A large, blotchy superficial discoloration due to hemorrhage into the tissues from ruptured blood vessels beneath the skin surface, without the skin itself being broken.

GLOSSARY OF MEDICAL TERMS

C

Carcinoma (Cancer)	A malignant tumour made up of connective tissue enclosing epithelial cells.
Cardiovascular	Pertaining to the heart (Cardio) and blood vessels (Vascular).
Cartilaginous	Consisting of cartilage (gristle).
Cavity	A hollow or space, especially a space within the body or one of its organs.
Cerebral	Pertaining to the cerebrum.
Cerebrum	The main portion of the brain occupying the upper part of the cranium.
Condyle	A rounded prominence or projection at the articular end of a bone.
Cornea	The clear, transparent anterior covering of the eye.

Corpuscle	Any small mass, organ or body.
Cortical Surface	The outer layer of an organ (Cortex), as distinguished from its inner substance (Medulla).
Cranium	The skeleton of the head.
Crown	The topmost part of an organ or structure.

D

Decomposition	The rotting or breaking down of body tissue.
Diaphragm	A dome shaped muscle separating the thoracic and abdominal cavities used for breathing.
Dissect	Cutting up of any organism or an organ for study.
Distal	Remote; farthest from any point of reference, as opposed to proximal.

Dorsal	Directed toward or situated on the back surface.
Duodenum	The first portion of the small intestine.
Dura Mater	The outermost, toughest and most fibrous of the three membranes covering the brain and spinal cord.

E

Epithelium	The covering of internal and external surfaces of the body, including the lining of vessels and other small cavities. It is made of cells held together by cementing material.
Erythrocytes	One of the cells found in blood (red blood cells) used for carrying oxygen to tissues.
Extrahepatic Biliary Tree	The bile ducts situated outside the liver, including gall bladder draining bile to the intestine.
Extracranial	Occurring outside of the cavities of the skull.

Extradural	Occurring outside the dura.

F

Faeces	The body waste discharged from the lower intestine. (Also referred to as excreta or excrement.)
Falx Cerebri	A small fold of dura mater in the posterior cranial fossa.
Foramen Magnum	A large natural opening at the base of the skull bone in the anterior port of the occipital bone connecting the spinal cord.
Frontal	Referring to the forehead.
Fracture	A break in the continuity of a bone.
Fossa	A pit or depression.

G

Gallbladder	A small saclike organ located below the liver that serves as a storage place for bile.
Gastric	Pertaining to the stomach.
Genitourinary	The organs of reproduction together with the organs concerned with production and excretion of urine.
Generative Organs	Organs pertaining to reproduction.
Gynecology	A branch of medicine that treats diseases of a woman's genital tract.

H

Hemorrhage	The escape of blood from a ruptured vessel.
Hematoma	An accumulation of free blood in the body anywhere.

GLOSSARY OF MEDICAL TERMS

Hepato-biliary	'Hepato' is pertaining to the liver whilst 'Biliary' is pertaining to the bile, to the bile ducts or to the gallbladder.
Histology	Microscopic study of the form and structure of the various tissues making up living organisms.
Hyoid Bone	A horseshoe shaped bone situated at the base of the tongue.

I

Intercellular	Between the cells.
Intestines	The membranous tube extending from the end of the stomach to the anus consisting of the small intestine and large intestine.
Intradernal	Within the substance of the skin.

GLOSSARY OF MEDICAL TERMS

Incision	A wound produced by a shape bladed instrument, eg., a surgeon's knife.
Infarct	An area of injured, dying and dead tissue produced by local lack of blood supply to the area due to obstruction or narrowing of blood vessels.
Infection	The invasion of body by an micro-organism and the tissue reaction to its presence.
Inferior	Located below or directed downward, mainly referring to the lower surface of organs.
Inflammation	Reaction of the body to any tissue injury, including toxin, micro-organism, trauma, etc.
Intercostal	Between the ribs.
Ischaemia	Lack of blood flowing into tissues or parts of organs due to functional constriction or actual blockage of a blood vessel.

GLOSSARY OF MEDICAL TERMS

J

Jaundice	Yellowness of skin and eyes caused by excess of bile pigment.
Jejunum	Part of the intestine from duodenum to the ileum.

L

Laceration	A wound produced by the tearing of body tissue (usually produced by blunt force application).
Larynx	The muscular and cartilaginous structure, lined with mucous membrane, situated at the top of the windpipe and below the root of the tongue.
Latent	Dormant or concealed.
Lateral	Pertaining to a side or farthest for the midline of a body.

GLOSSARY OF MEDICAL TERMS

Lesions	Any damage to a tissue, including wounds, sores, ulcers, tumours, cataracts and other tissue damage.
Leukaemia	A cancer originating from the precursors of blood forming cells.
Leukocytes	A cell found in the blood mainly used for defence against any foreign material introduced into the body (white blood cells).
Ligature	A thread or wire used in surgery to tie off blood vessels to prevent bleeding or strangulating a body part.
Liver	A large gland of red colour located in the upper right portion of the abdomen that produces bile which helps to detoxify harmful substances in the blood and stores food.
Lividity	A purple discoloration of the body after death due to gravitation of blood to the dependent sides of the body.
Lumen	The cavity or channel within a tube or tubular organ.

Lymph Node	Lymph nodes filter and destroy invading bacteria and are the site of production of lymphocytes (one of the white blood cells).
Lymphadenopathy	Disease of the lymph nodes.

M

Medial	Pertaining to the middle, closer to the midline of a body.
Medial Epicondyle	Pertaining to or situated toward the midline of an eminence or projection above the condyle of a bone.
Membrane	A thin layer of tissue that covers a surface or divides an organ.
Mediastinum	The mass of tissues and organs separating the two lungs between the sternum in front, the vertebral column at the back, the thoracic inlet at the top and the diaphragm at the bottom. It contains the heart and its great vessels, the trachea, oesophagus and other structures and tissues. It is divided into the anterior, the middle, the superior and the inferior regions.

GLOSSARY OF MEDICAL TERMS

Mesentery	A membranous fold attaching the intestine to the abdominal wall.
Midline	A perpendicular line that divides a body into two equal halves.
Musculomembranous	Pertaining to muscle and membrane.
Mucosa	Mucous membrane.
Myocardium	The muscular substance of the heart.

N

Nasal	Pertaining to the nose.
Necrosis	Death of tissue usually in a small, localised area.

GLOSSARY OF MEDICAL TERMS

O

Oedema	An abdominal accumulation of fluid in the intercellular spaces of the body.
Oesophagus	The hollow muscular tube extending from the pharynx to the stomach.
Occipital Region	Pertaining to the back of the head.
Omentum	A fold of peritoneum extending from the stomach to adjacent abdominal organs.
Orbit	The boney cavity containing the eyeball and its associated muscles, vessels and nerves.
Organ	A somewhat independent part of the body that serves a specific function or functions.
Orifice	The entrance or outlet of any body cavity.

GLOSSARY OF MEDICAL TERMS

P

Pancreas	A large gland located below the stomach and the liver.
Parietal	Of or pertaining to the walls of a cavity, eg., pleural or peritoneal cavities.
Parietal Bone	One of two quadrilateral bones forming the sides and roof of the skull bone.
Patent	Open, obstructed or not closed.
Pelvis	The basin formed by the hipbones and lower portion of the vertebral column constituting the lowest part of the trunk.
Pericardium	The fibroserous sac enclosing the heart.
Peritoneum	The serous membrane lining the walls of the abdominal and pelvic cavities and investing containing viscera, the two layers enclosing a potential space, the peritoneal cavity.

GLOSSARY OF MEDICAL TERMS

Petechial	A small, pinpoint, non-raised, perfectly round, purplish red spot caused by haemorrage under the skin or under the mucosa.
Pneumonia	Inflammation of the lung tissue.
Pharynx	The musculomembranous cavity behind the nasal cavities, mouth and laryx communicating with them and with the oesophagus.
Portal Vein	A short thick vein formed by the union of two veins behind the neck of the pancreas that drains blood from the intestine to the liver for cleaning.
Posterior	Directed toward or situated at the back.
Postero-lateral	Situated on the side and toward the back.
Pulmonary Parenchyma	Pertaining to the lung tissue.
Putrefaction	Decomposition of the body effected largely by action of micro-organisms.

Pylorus	The junction of the stomach and the duodenum.

R

Rectum	The distal portion of the large intestine ending in the anus.
Renal	Pertaining to the kidney.
Respiration	The exchange of oxygen and carbon dioxide in the lungs between the cell and its environment and in the metabolism of the cell.
Respiratory	Pertaining to respiration.
Rigid	Inflexible or stiff.
Rigor Mortis	Rigidity of skeletal muscles developing 6 to 10 hours after death and persisting for 3 to 4 days.

GLOSSARY OF MEDICAL TERMS

S

Scalp	That part of the skin covering the skull bone that is covered with hair.
Sphenoid Bone	An irregular wedge-shaped bone at the end of the skull.
Spinal Cord	The part of the central nervous system lodged in the spinal canal.
Spleen	A large gland-like organ situated under the ribs on the left side of the upper abdomen.
Sternum	A place of bone forming the middle of the anterior wall of the thorax and articulating with the clavicles and the cartilages of the first seven ribs.
Subdural	Beneath the dural mater.
Supine	Lying with the face upward or in the dorsal surface.
Suprarenal glands	Glands above the kidney.

GLOSSARY OF MEDICAL TERMS

Suppuration	Formation or discharge of pus.

T

Thorax	The part of the body between the neck and abdomen.
Thrombosis	Formation of blood clots inside a blood vessel or in one of the chambers of the heart.
Thymus	A two-lobed ductless gland situated behind the upper part of the sternum and extending into the neck usually seen in children.
Thyroid Cartilage	The shield-shaped cartilage of the larynx, the prominence it produces on the neck is the Adam's apple.
Toxicology	The science or study of poisons.
Trachea	The air passage extending from the throat and larynx to the main bronchi. (Also referred to as the windpipe.)

Trunk	The main part of a body to which the head and limbs are attached.

U

Urethea	The canal extending from the bladder and opening to the outside of the body.
Urinary	Pertaining to the urine.
Urine	The fluid containing water and waste products that stored in the bladder and discharged by the kidneys by way of the urethra.

V

Vagina	The canal of the female from the external genitalia to the cervix.
Vaginal Fornices	A recess formed between vaginal wall and the vaginal part of the cervix. (Also referred to as posterior fornix, anterior fornix or lateral fornices.)

GLOSSARY OF MEDICAL TERMS

Vein	A vessel through which blood passes from various organs back to the heart.
Vena Cava	The veins that return blood from the upper and lower parts of the body to the heart.
Ventricle	A small cavity or chamber as in the brain or heart.
Viscera	Any large interior organ in any of the great body cavities, especially those in the abdomen.

Sources: Encyclopedia and Dictionary of Medicine and Nursing, 1972, B. F. Miller MD and C. B. K RN, BS, M Ed (eds.), W. B. Saunders Co. and Dr. P. Golpak, Pathologist, Port Moresby General Hospital.

APPENDICES

APPENDIX 1

INITIAL REPORT OF DEATH TO CORONER

APPENDICES

INITIAL REPORT OF DEATH TO CORONER

DEATH OF ....

1. TIME AND DATE OF DEATH: ....

2. WHERE DEATH TOOK PLACE: ....

3. BY WHOM REPORTED: ....

4. WHEN REPORTED: ....

5. BY WHOM LAST SEEN ALIVE: ....

6. WHEN LAST SEEN ALIVE: ....

7. WHERE LAST SEEN ALIVE: ....

8. ANY SUSPICIOUS CIRCUMSTANCES: ....

9. DATE OF BIRTH AND AGE OF DECEASED: ....

10. PLACE OF BIRTH: ....

11. MARITAL STATUS: ....

12. OCCUPATION: ....

13. ADDRESS: ....

14. DETAILS OF NEXT OF KIN: ....

    ....

15. HOW WAS THE IDENTIFICATION OF THE DECEASED CONFIRMED:

    ....

    ....

16. IS A HOMICIDAL OFFENCE BEING INVESTIGATED: ....

17. DETAILS OF THE PROPERTY OF THE DECEASED TAKEN POSSESSION OF:

    ....

    ....

    ....

    ....

APPENDICES

18. BRIEF CIRCUMSTANCES UNDER WHICH THE DEATH TOOK PLACE, INCLUDING ANY PRIOR LIFE-THREATENING ILLNESS, IF KNOWN:

....

....

....

....

....

....

....

....

....

....

....

....

....

....

....

....

....

....

....

SIGNATURE: ....

NAME AND RANK OF INVESTIGATING OFFICER: ....

DATE: ....

APPENDICES

APPENDIX 2

INITIAL REPORT OF FIRE TO CORONER

APPENDICES

INITIAL REPORT OF FIRE TO CORONER

1. TIME AND DATE OF FIRE: ....

2. LOCATION OF FIRE: ....

3. BY WHOM REPORTED: ....

4. WHEN REPORTED: ....

5. ARE THERE ANY SUSPICIOUS CIRCUMSTANCES: YES / NO

6. IS THE OFFENCE OF ARSON BEING INVESTIGATED: YES / NO

7. SUMMARY OF THE PROPERTY LOST IN THE FIRE:

   ....

   ....

   ....

   ....

   ....

   ....

   ....

   ....

8. ESTIMATE OF VALUE OF PROPERTY LOST IN THE FIRE: K..

9. DID ANY PERSON DIE, IF SO PROVIDE THEIR DETAILS:

   ....

   ....

   ....

10. WAS ANY PERSON INJURED, IF SO PROVIDE THEIR DETAILS:

   ....

   ....

   ....

11. **BRIEF CIRCUMSTANCES OF THE FIRE:**

....

....

....

....

....

....

....

....

....

....

....

....

....

....

....

....

....

....

SIGNATURE: ....

NAME AND RANK: ....

DATE: ....

INDEX

Page

A

Appointment -- Coroner 19

B

Burial 55

C

Comments -- Coronial Inquest 141

Competency And Compellability -- Witness In A Coronial Inquest 94

Contempt Of Court -- Coronial Inquest 145

Coroner -- Appointment 19

Coroner's Assistant -- Role In A Coronial Inquest 86

Court Procedure 75

- Competency And Compellability 94
- Coroner's Assistant 86
- Examination Of Witnesses 99
- Interested Party 88
- Media 79
- Oath, Solemn Declaration And Affirmation 93
- Open Court 78
- Privilege Against Self-Incrimination 97
- Protection Of Witnesses 98
- Rules Of Evidence 81
- Rules Of Natural Justice 83

INDEX

Page

Statements And Reports 104

D

Death

Initial Report 28

Investigation 32

Investigation File 34

Death Inquest 21

Comments And Recommendations 142

Findings 112

Findings -- Accidental Death 119

Findings -- Death Uncertain 113

Findings -- Killed Lawfully 127

Findings -- Killed Unlawfully 124

Findings -- Misadventure 122

Findings -- Natural Causes 115

Findings -- Neglect 117

Findings -- No Death 113

Findings -- Open Finding 113

Findings -- Suicide 115

Findings -- Traffic Accident 123

Jurisdiction 23

Witness Competency And Compellability 94

INDEX

	Page
Death In Custody	40
Avoidable Harm	45
Brutality	45
Duty Of Care	44
Investigation	42
E	
Examination Of Witnesses -- Coronial Inquest	99
Exhibits -- Coronial Inquest	144
Exhumation	56
F	
Findings	106
Death Inquest	112
Death Inquest -- Accidental Death	119
Death Inquest -- Death Uncertain	113
Death Inquest -- Killed Lawfully	127
Death Inquest -- Killed Unlawfully	124
Death Inquest -- Misadventure	122
Death Inquest -- Natural Causes	115
Death Inquest -- Neglect	118
Death Inquest -- No Death	113
Death Inquest -- Open Finding	113
Death Inquest -- Suicide	115

INDEX

	Page
Death Inquest -- Traffic Accident	123
Fire Inquest	135
Missing Person Inquest	137
Standard Of Proof	110
Fire Inquest	58
Findings	135
Witness Competency And Compellability	94

G

Glossary Of Medical Terms	153

I

Identification	45
Dental Records	47
Distinctive Markings	47
DNA Test	48
Fingerprints	47
Methods	46
Personal Identification Documentation	49
Personal Property	48
X-Rays	48
Initial Report	
Death	28
Fire	61

INDEX

	Page
Initial Report Of Death To Coroner form	175
Initial Report Of Fire To Coroner form	178
Interested Party	88
Investigating Officer's Statement	
Death Inquest	38
Fire Inquest	66
Missing Person Inquest	70
Investigation	
Death	32
Fire	62
Investigation File	
Death Inquest	34
Fire Inquest	63
Missing Person Inquest	68

J

Judicial Review	147

M

Media – Coronial Inquest	79
Missing Person Inquest	67
Findings	137
Witness Competency And Compellability	96

INDEX

	Page
N	
No Death Inquest	25
Non-suspicious Death	31
Non-unusual Death	31
O	
Oath, Solemn Declaration And Affirmation -- Coronial Inquest	93
Open Court -- Coronial Inquest	78
P	
Post-Mortem Examination	49
Protection Of Witnesses	98
R	
Recommendations -- Coronial Inquest	141
Re-Opening -- Coronial Inquest	146
Rules Of Evidence -- Coronial Inquest	81
Rules Of Natural Justice -- Coronial Inquest	83
S	
Standard Of Proof -- Findings	110
V	
View -- Body Of Deceased	31

INDEX

Page

W

Witness

Attendance 71

Competency And Compellability 94

Oath, Solemn Declaration And Affirmation 93

Privilege Against Self-Incrimination 97

Protection 98

Statements And Reports 104